In addition to knowing the code names of all the plays and formations and the roles of everyone on his own team, the quarterback has to be able to come up to the line of scrimmage, take a second or two to scan the defense, and recognize what formation the defense is in and then process the information through his brain like a high-speed computer. Then he has to decide whether to stay with the play that was called because it should work against the defense he's looking at, or to change the play by calling an audible—an entirely different play or formation called out to his team at the line of scrimmage—because the play that was called won't work against the defensive formation that he sees. The quarterback has to see and decide all this in seconds, and he has to know the plays and formations and assignments so well that he can do it as automatically as he would cross a street when the light turns green.

JOHN ELWAY ★ BERNIE KOSAR

RICHARD J. BRENNER

LYNX BOOKS
New York

JOHN ELWAY * BERNIE KOSAR

ISBN: 1-55802-331-3

First Printing / September 1988

Cover photos: Mitchell B. Reibel/Sportschrome

This book is published by Lynx Books, a division of Lynx
Communications, Inc., 41 Madison Avenue, New York,
New York, 10010. The name "Lynx" together with the
logotype consisting of a stylized head of a lynx is a trade-
mark of Lynx Communications, Inc.

Printed in the United States of America

0 9 8 7 6 5 4 3 2 1

Dedication

With great love for Jason and Halle, my superstar children, and Anita, my wife and chief researcher.

Thank you for all your encouragement, advice, and assistance. And with love, too, for my very special mother.

For Lou Wolfe, with real respect and fondness.

And special thanks to Rich Mauch of the NFL; Brent Emmett of the Boardman *Bugle;* Lynda Nemeroff; Lynne Brummond; Dick Sugarman; John Galetka; Donald Katzman; Bette Lipsky; Ron Wilson and Dale Schmidt.

And for Judy, Stan, Peter, Richard, and Lisa Makover for being so wonderfully accommodating.

The author wishes to acknowledge the following:

The New York Times
Sport magazine
Sports Illustrated magazine
Newsweek
Newsday
The New York Post
The Bugle, The Boardman High School newspaper

Introduction

Today, John Elway and Bernie Kosar are two of the best quarterbacks in the NFL. But their paths to glory were as different as their talents and personalities.

John was recognized as an exceptional athlete when he was very young. He was an all-American football player and a draft selection by the Kansas City Royals baseball team while he was still in high school. He went on to become an all-American at Stanford University and to play baseball for a New York Yankee farm team.

From the beginning, it had always been easy for John. But his first few years in the NFL brought him his first taste of failure. For three years John's performances never quite measured up to the expectations that he had inspired. But he faced up to the adversity and overcame the disappointments to twice lead Denver to the Super Bowl.

Bernie Kosar is not a great natural athlete. Even when he was in grade school, people said that he was too slow. But Bernie always had great determination and confidence in his own abilities.

He began his career at the University of Miami as the third-string quarterback and wound up leading the Hurricanes to the national championship.

Bernie has led the Cleveland Browns into the playoffs in each of his three seasons in the NFL, while in the last two AFC Championship games, he and John have lit the fuse on two of the most exciting and explosive play-off games ever played.

It is highly likely that the paths of these two superstars will continue to cross and will continue, like live wires, to send sparks flashing through professional football.

1

JOHN ELWAY

1

The Living Is Easy

John Albert Elway was born June 28, 1960, in Port Angeles, Washington. He spent his earliest years in Washington and Montana, where the family moved when his father, a football coach, changed jobs.

John displayed exceptional athletic ability at a very early age, and he always received a lot of encouragement and coaching from his father and mother, Jack and Janet. Jack had been a fine quarterback himself until an injury in college had ended his career. John's grandfather, Harry Elway, had also been a quarterback and had played against the great Jim Thorpe.

When he was three years old, John picked up a plastic baseball bat and began swinging. His father, thinking ahead to a time when John would be facing curveballs, walked over and showed John how to swing like a lefty. This would give John an advantage in the future, because most pitchers, like most people, are right-handed.

The Elway family, John notes, "has always been very competitive. When we were young, my dad would time us in races in putting on our pajamas. My mom and sisters, Jana and Lee Ann, are real competitors too. We play games, but we play to win."

Even before John took up football, he was always throwing things. "Dirt clods, snowballs, stones, just about anything. I'd set up bottles on a fence and knock them down all day long. I loved to throw."

John showed so much early promise at throwing a football that when Jack accepted a coaching job in the Los Angeles area, the first thing that he checked out, even before the family went looking for a house, was which high school in the area had the best football program. He finally settled on Grenada Hills High School, which

5

had a fine football program that used a pro-style passing attack and threw the ball about forty times per game. The year-round program helped John to develop technique and arm strength. "We threw all summer long," John recalls. "In my first two years of high school I got more experience than most guys get after two years of college. The experience of throwing a football when you're young is so much more important than trying to learn and memorize what to do."

That experience and practice, combined with John's natural ability, paid off big in his junior year as he threw for an eye-popping 3,039 yards and 25 touchdowns. Jack Neumeier, his high-school coach, remembers, "He had that great ability to see the whole field and not only focus on the primary receiver. I knew he could be a pro after his junior year."

His father also noticed John's exceptional ability to see what was happening all over the field. "I first saw that vision when he was young, playing basketball. He could see everything on the court. I was always the first to quit in whatever we played. Man, he was *fun*."

In the spring John proved to be as adept at baseball as he had been at football. He compiled a .551 batting average while earning all-city honors and leading his team to the city championship.

In his senior year of football he threw for 1,837 yards and 19 TD's before a knee injury brought his season to an abrupt conclusion after only five games.

John recovered in time to play in the Shrine All-star Game and led the North squad, with his father coaching, to a lopsided 35–15 victory. John set two records and tied another while putting on a dazzling performance.

He completed 23 passes in 37 attempts, good for 363 yards and four TD's, and was voted the MVP in the game. He was also selected as a high school all-American by *Parade, Scholastic Coach, Football News,* The National Coaches' Association, and the Joe Namath magazine, *Prep All-America*, and was the most highly recruited football player in America.

Before going on to college, though, John had another season of baseball to enjoy. He ripped opposing pitching for a .491 average as a right fielder with a rifle arm. And as a part-time pitcher, he was 4–2 with a nifty 1.03 ERA. During the play-offs he hit a scintillating .692, which earned him the tournament MVP award. Grenada beat Crenshaw High in Dodger Stadium in the final game as John came on in relief to nail down a 10–4 victory with one-hit relief work. Crenshaw's big bat belonged to Darryl Strawberry, currently the star right fielder of the New York Mets. John threw smoke at Darryl and got him to hit a harmless pop-up to left field.

John ended an amazing high school athletic career by being named to the all-City team again and voted the Southern California Baseball Player of the Year.

John was recruited to play football by more than seventy colleges. He narrowed his choice to two schools in the PAC-10 conference, USC and Stanford, and finally decided on the Cardinals because Stanford was the only school that encouraged him to also play baseball. Jack Elway had been named the head coach at San Jose State, which is only twenty minutes away from Stanford. He would have loved to have had John play for him, but he never pressured John. "I didn't want to interfere with his dream of playing in the PAC-10, but it still bothers me that I had the best prospect in the country sitting across from me at the breakfast table and I let him slip through my fingers."

Another reason for choosing Stanford was that the school has a tradition of turning out great quarterbacks, like John Brodie, Steve Dils, and Jim Plunkett.

John saw only limited action in his first year because senior Turk Schonert, another one of those great Stanford quarterbacks, was the leading college passer in the nation in 1979. But he saw enough action to pass for more than 500 yards and set a new Stanford record for freshmen by throwing six TD passes. He showed so much promise with his passing and scrambling skills that the fans and the coaching staff knew they had something special to look forward to.

7

As the next football season got under way, John more than delivered on the potential that he had displayed in his freshman year. In just the fourth game of his sophomore season, he rocketed to national attention when he led the Cardinals to a shocking 31–14 upset victory over the heavily favored University of Oklahoma, which was ranked as the number three college team in the country. John was a one-man wrecking crew as he ran for one TD and threw for three more while completing 20 of 34 attempts for 237 yards. After the game Barry Switzer, the head coach of the stunned Sooners, said, "That was the greatest exhibition of quarterback play I have ever seen on this field."

John even impressed coaches when Stanford lost. John Robinson, currently the coach of the Los Angeles Rams and who had desperately tried to recruit John for USC, said, "John Elway is one of the all-time greats. I compare him to Roger Staubach." And that was right after Robinson's Trojans had trounced the Cardinals 34–9!

When John returned to Washington to play Washington State, he left behind a memory that they wouldn't easily forget. Playing an almost perfect game, he completed 29 of 36 passes for 379 yards and five TD's, and also rushed for one. Just to show he had nothing personal against Washington, he tied an NCAA record the following week against Oregon State by throwing four TD passes in the first quarter. He finished up the day with a total of six TD tosses and a one-way ticket to anywhere else from the Oregon State coaching staff.

John also led the Cardinals to a 35–21 victory over his dad's team, San Jose State. John threw for three TD's in the victory against the Spartans, but they had the distinction of holding him to "only" 167 yards passing, the one time that season that he failed to throw for more than 200 yards.

When the season was over and the numbers were added up, they told a remarkable story. In his first season as a starter, John had tied one NCAA record, most touchdown passes in a quarter, and set six PAC-10 records, including: completed passes—248; TD passes—27; TD's responsible for (both rushing and passing)—31;

and total offense (rushing and passing yardage combined)—2,939. John also racked up 2,889 yards passing, the second best mark in PAC-10 history, and demonstrated awesome accuracy by completing 65.4 percent of his passes.

His sensational season did not go unrewarded. He became the first sophomore quarterback in eighteen years to gain all-American honors, and he became the first soph ever to win the PAC-10 Player of the Year award.

John didn't have much time to admire his trophies; he barely had time to pick up his awards and change his football helmet for a baseball cap.

John made up for a disappointing freshman campaign, in which he had hit only .269, with a vengeance in his second season by whacking opposing pitchers for a .361 average while crashing nine home runs and knocking in 50 runs in 49 games. He went on to hit a torrid .444 while leading the Cardinals to a runner-up finish in the NCAA Central Regional Tournament. John's hitting and outstanding outfield play earned him All-NCAA Tournament First Team honors by unanimous selection.

College baseball pitchers and coaches slept a little bit easier when it was announced on September 19 that John had signed a minor-league contract to play baseball the following summer for the New York Yankees. Yankee Vice President Bill Bergesch echoed the thoughts of the entire organization when he said, "We feel that John Elway has the rare ability to move to the Big Leagues in a hurry. I envision him playing right field for the New York Yankees in just a couple of years if he wants to."

Signing a professional baseball contract meant that John was ineligible to play any more college baseball, but he was still free to terrorize opponents on the gridiron.

John had begun his junior year with a bang by blasting the Boilermakers of Purdue for a career high of 33 completions (in 44 attempts) good for 418 yards, despite suffering a sprained ankle in the second half. Unfortunately for Stanford, John's heroics weren't sufficient, though, and the Cardinals went down to defeat 27–19.

In the next game, against San Jose State (the team coached by his dad), John went from bang to bust as he limped through his poorest collegiate performance. He posted career-worst totals as he completed only six passes in 24 attempts for 72 yards, and was intercepted five times and sacked seven times. John also failed to throw a TD pass (the only time that would happen during the season), which ended his streak at 12 consecutive games. Stanford, needless to say, lost the game, 24–6.

While John was trying to concentrate on football, fans and reporters kept questioning him about whether he was going to play right field for the New York Yankees or quarterback an NFL team. The questioning was so constant that, as John said, "Sometimes I feel like strangling the next person who asks The Big Question. Right now I'm just trying to do well at football."

John did better than well—he dazzled. Against the much stronger Ohio State Buckeyes, ranked as the number eight team in the country, John completed 21 of his last 27 passes. His two fourth-quarter TD tosses fell just short of pulling off a major upset.

John also threw a second-half scare into the seventh-ranked Trojans of USC by hitting 17 of 30 passes for 199 yards and two TD's. Against Arizona State, John was awesome. He passed for 270 yards and three TD tosses before he was forced out of the game with injuries less than halfway through the *second quarter*.

John got even better as the season wore down, as he threw 15 TD tosses in the last six games, including at two-TD, 361-yard passing effort against Washington—the team that went on to win the Rose Bowl.

Except for San Jose State and Arizona, *no one* stopped John. But his acrobatic accomplishments couldn't entirely compensate for a weak supporting cast, however, and the Cardinals finished at 4–7, their worst season since 1963. While Stanford slumped, John soared, and his spectacular performances drew raves from the NFL.

Dick Steinberg, the highly respected personnel director of the New England Patriots, didn't hesitate in giving his opinion about

John. "John Elway is the best quarterback prospect I've ever seen. He is the best player in college football today. He has *no* flaws."

Dallas Cowboy Vice President Gil Brandt was equally enthusiastic. "If he was a senior, he'd be the first guy picked in the draft. Even though we have Danny White, and even if we also had Dan Fouts and Joe Montana, I'd still draft John Elway."

Bill Walsh, the coach and president of the San Francisco 49ers, a man not usually given over to exaggeration, also put his seal of approval on John. "He's probably the best college quarterback I've ever seen."

The next stop on John's athletic odyssey, however, was not an NFL city, but Oneonta, a little town in upstate New York. John had accepted George Steinbrenner's offer—including about $140,000—to spend six weeks during the summer of 1982 playing professional baseball for the Oneonta Yankees, a Class A minor-league team.

John was a bit anxious at the beginning. He hadn't played competitive baseball in more than a year, and he "didn't want to go someplace and flop." And getting off to a slow start didn't help those anxious feelings. He went hitless in his first three games, and after eight games he was only three for 27 batting a lowly .111. What's more, his right arm, the arm that threw the touchdown passes, had tightened up. John wasn't feeling very happy. He had a touch of homesickness, and he was worried about the ache in his arm and his lack of hitting. Calling home eased the first problem. When he spoke to his father, he joked, "Dad, I think my goal is to hit .100." His father offered encouragement and reassurance, and told him, "Be aware of your mistakes, but don't let them crush you." Participating in a good warm-up before each workout took care of the stiffness in his arm, and John's concern about his anemic batting average was put to rest by Yankee official Bill Bergesch. Bill told him to just keep playing and not to worry—the hits would start to come.

There was an old problem that John couldn't work out—the constant hounding by fans and reporters who wanted to know the answer to The Big Question. As Ken Berry, the manager of the Oneonta team, observed, "He wasn't here three days and there was a bunch of sportswriters asking him stupid questions."

John was very patient, though, and explained over and over that it was too soon for him to make a decision and that he loved playing both sports. "It's a seasonal thing. I enjoy football in football season and baseball in baseball season. But I'd stop either one if they stopped being fun."

One of the reasons that John liked baseball was that he felt less pressure than he did when he played quarterback. "Standing out in right field, it's a relief to know that the whole world isn't revolving about me." And he loved the feeling of making long throws from the outfield. "I love to take two steps into a fly ball and then hum it home, just let it fly and watch it move."

Back in California, Jack Elway was concerned that his son would think too much about the future and miss out on the pure pleasure of playing. "I've seen it with kids I've coached. The only thing they're thinking about is who to sign with. John is about to start his last year of college athletics, and I want him to enjoy it to the fullest. He doesn't have to make a decision now. He doesn't have to give it a thought until the football season is over."

Back on the field John straightened his stroke and started to swat opposing pitchers. By the end of his six-week season he had raised his average to .318 and had a team-leading 24 RBI's, and no errors in 42 games. John had really enjoyed playing baseball, but as he packed his bags his thoughts were already three thousand miles away. "I'm not a goal setter," he told a reporter, "but whatever it takes to get us to the Rose Bowl is what I want to do this year. I want to have some fun, win some games, and go to a bowl game."

Stanford won their season opener, and John definitely had some fun, connecting on 29 of 36 pass attempts for 333 yards and four TD's as he led the Cardinals past Purdue 35–14 in a nationally televised game. Afterward Leon Burtnett, the Boilermaker coach, said, "I consider him to be the best quarterback in history at the college level."

John had some more fun at the expense of another Big Ten team when the Cardinals traveled to Columbus to play Ohio State. The Buckeyes were leading with less than a minute to go when John zipped a cross-field pass that won the game and gave John 407 yards passing for the day. After the game the Ohio State coach, Earle Bruce, said, "He's as good as anybody I've ever seen."

John kept putting on prime performances, as he did against Oregon State, when he threw for 381 yards and five TD's. Against undefeated and top-ranked Washington, John connected on 20 of 30 passes for 265 yards and two TD's as he led Stanford to a stunning upset. After the game Don James, the disappointed coach of the Huskies, said that the reason for the loss was simple: "We didn't win today because we weren't able to stop Elway."

John was almost unstoppable, but Stanford wasn't a dominant team, so despite John's efforts, the defeats mounted as quickly as the victories. One of the losses was a 35–31 scorcher against San Jose State. The Elway family was glad that John and his dad wouldn't be competing against each other anymore. "It was a terrible, wrenching experience," explained John's mom, Janet. "We never knew whether to laugh or cry at the end, so we always did both. We're just relieved that the whole thing is over and we don't have to do it again."

John's dream of a bowl bid for Stanford died in the last four seconds of the last game of the season, when the University of California ran back a kickoff for the winning touchdown. It was an incredible play that involved *five* laterals and the unintentional interference of the Stanford marching band that was on the field prematurely because they thought the game had ended. A few days later John was still feeling the loss. "We had converted a fourth and seventeen and kicked what looked like the winning field goal. It still hurts having a bowl game snatched from your hands with four seconds left."

John's final season ended disappointingly, but his college career had been spectacular. He finished with 9,349 yards passing, 77 touchdown passes, and a pageful of records, including 17 PAC-10

13

passing records and five NCAA passing records. But more than the records, John had left an indelible impression of his unique skills. Darryl Rogers, who at the time was the coach of Arizona State, spoke for a lot of people when he said, "There's probably never been anyone who's had a greater impact on the game of college football. He may be the best quarterback in the history of NCAA football."

John was finally going to have to answer The Big Question. Would it be baseball or football? It was obvious to a lot of people that John preferred to play in the NFL. He had even told some people that he would rather play football if he could play for a West Coast team, close to home. He was a solid prospect as a baseball player and might—in two or three years—reach the major leagues. But as a football player, he was rated as the number one prospect in the country, certain to be the first player selected in the NFL draft of college players.

The problem was that the Baltimore Colts, by virtue of their last-place finish, had the first pick in the 1983 draft. John and his dad made it perfectly clear that John wouldn't sign with the Colts. They didn't like the owner, Robert Irsay, or the coach, Frank Kush. They told Colt officials that if they didn't trade the pick to another team, preferably a West Coast team, John would forget football and sign with the New York Yankees.

The Colts did hold trade talks with a number of very interested teams, but they finally decided to pick John and hoped that they could get him to change his mind.

Jack Elway was furious. "Three times we told Kush that John wouldn't play for the Colts. They don't seem to understand English. We know that the Chargers and Raiders made excellent offers for the first pick, and we can't understand why the Colts turned them down."

John was angry and frustrated. "I'm bewildered right now. I don't know where I am, but I know that I'll never play in Baltimore."

The problem was resolved a few days later when Robert Irsay, the president of the Colts, decided that something was better than nothing, and traded John to the Denver Broncos in return for Chris Hinton, an offensive tackle and the fourth selection in the draft; Mark Herrmann, a back-up quarterback; and Denver's first pick in the following year's draft.

When the owner of the Colts made the announcement, there was smoke coming out of his ears. "Elway got his way, but he didn't get his way. He wanted to play on the West Coast, and we put him five hundred miles away. He'll never be any good."

Irsay wasn't the only person to express hard feelings. A lot of people felt that John had acted like a spoiled brat. They believed that he should have been willing to play for whatever team drafted him, regardless of his own feelings. Terry Bradshaw, the Steelers' great quarterback, was outspoken in his criticism. "He ought to grow up and pay his dues." There were other people, though, who felt that John had every right to try to make the system work for his benefit.

John was stung by the criticism, but mainly he was relieved that the situation was resolved. "I didn't have anything against the city of Baltimore; I just didn't want to play for Irsay or Coach Kush. Kush is a military type. I wouldn't even take a free recruiting trip to Arizona State when I was in high school and he was the coach there." Interestingly enough, Kush was fired by Irsay after one more season, and the following year Irsay spirited the Colts to Indianapolis.

John went to Denver and quickly signed a five-year, 5-million-dollar contract, which made him the highest-paid player in the history of the league.

From his early days as a high school all-American to his glory days at Stanford, John had always been a natural, a superstar. In a year that produced what many experts consider to be the most talented crop of college seniors in NFL history, John was the number one pick, ahead of Eric Dickerson, Tony Eason, Jim Kelly, and Dan Marino—ahead of everybody. And before he had taken his first NFL snap or thrown his first NFL pass, he was already its highest-paid player. He truly was the golden boy of the California dream.

2

A Rocky Road

"I'm starting at the bottom again," said John prior to the preseason. "I realize that Denver was two and seven last year and some people want to throw me in there. But Coach Reeves wants to bring me along slowly. I'm glad I'm not walking into a situation where I'm starting the first game. That would be a lot of pressure. I'm just going to do my best and let what happens happen. I've got some things to learn." But no one really wanted to wait for John. Everyone wanted Instant Elway.

The day after John signed, *The Denver Post* carried thirteen stories on him, and the competing *Rocky Mountain News* carried six. When John reported to training camp, both newspapers began daily columns known as "The Elway Watch," and each day they would fill them with details of John's day: *fascinating* items such as "John threw 97 passes in practice today" and what he had eaten for lunch. The Denver fans were hungry for a winner, and the newspapers, along with TV and radio, served John up every day as the main course.

John had gotten used to media attention at Stanford, but that didn't prepare him for the daily crush of reporters who wanted to interview him every day, all day long. It was extremely distracting, which made things difficult for a rookie quarterback still trying to learn his assignments. It was also ridiculous that so much attention had been given to one person. John was the first to admit, "There's been a lot blown out of proportion. I've been a little overcovered."

"I thought Joe Namath got a lot of press and publicity when he was a rookie," said Bronco publicist Charlie Lee, "but it was nothing in comparison to what Elway got. After the first scrimmage of the year, we had a fifteen-minute autograph session. The people just engulfed him like he was meat thrown to piranha. We had to have three security men get him off the field.''

John fed the fans' frenzy by putting on a superstar performance in his first NFL preseason action. He took the field in the second half against Seattle, and while nearly 54,000 Broncomaniacs in Mile High Stadium roared their approval, John riddled the Seahawk defense as if it were a pickup group. He drove Denver to the go-ahead touchdown by completing five of six passes in a ten-play, 75-yard drive. John had demonstrated his enormous ability by throwing ''ropes'' into double coverages and scrambling for first downs. After the game he reminded people, ''I've got a long way to go and a lot to learn.'' But no one was listening.

Sports Illustrated sent a reporter and a photographer to cover the game. The following week John was on the cover of the magazine. In the story the author, after having watched just the one preseason effort, wrote, ''If he keeps this up, he'll be a legend by September. . . .''

After two more preseason performances, Coach John Reeves decided that he had seen enough, and announced that John would be the starter on opening day instead of the veteran Steve DeBerg. ''It's his job until he can't handle it. But I feel confident he will handle it from the start.'' Reeves just oozed with praise for his rookie quarterback. ''There's not many people with his kind of talent. He's just got a super arm. He has great velocity and accuracy, and he puts it where he aims it. He has great football instincts and a great future.'' Reeves had looked at John—at the powerful arm and the quick feet—and had been dazzled by the talent and the confidence with which he played the game. Reeves had seen the future, and its name was Elway.

John had also decided that he was ready. ''It's not really as big a jump to the pros as people say it is. I'm not overwhelmed by the difference in talent. I understand the game. I know what it's about.''

He had looked sensational against the rookies and free agents and the ''vanilla'' defenses that he had faced in the preseason

17

games. They're called "vanilla" because they're basic: no nuts or raisins, no 250-pound blitzing linebackers coming at your face off a stunt with the defensive end while the backs rotate their zone coverage away from where they showed it right before the snap of the ball. But when the regular season began, the regular NFL defenders came out to play, and John just wasn't prepared.

Playing quarterback in the NFL isn't as simple as it seems from the stands or from watching it on TV. It's not just a question of calling a play, taking the snap from the center and then handing off or throwing the ball. A quarterback first has to learn an entire new code language so that he can call the proper play *and* the proper formation from which it should be run. The same exact play can be run from different formations, and players will have different assignments to carry out depending upon the play selection and the formation from which it is run. The quarterback also has to know what each of his ten teammates is supposed to do on each play and in each formation. And he also has to remember what the snap count is on each play and to keep changing it so that the defense can't time its charge.

In addition to knowing the code names of all the plays and formations and the roles of everyone on his own team, the quarterback has to be able to come up to the line of scrimmage, take a second or two to scan the defense, and recognize what formation the defense is in—are they, for example, playing zone or man-to-man in the backfield? Are they double-covering any receivers? Who has drawn single coverage? Is a linebacker or two going to blitz? Are they more vulnerable to a pass or a running play?—and then process the information through his brain like a high-speed computer. Then he has to decide whether to stay with the play that was called because it should work against the defense he's looking at, or to change the play by calling an audible—an entirely different play or formation called out to his team at the line of scrimmage—because the play that was called won't work against the defensive formation that he sees. The quarterback has to see and decide all this in seconds, and he has to know the plays and formations and assignments so well that he can do it as automatically as he would cross a street when the light turns green.

Because there is so much to learn and because the quarterback directs the entire offense, it is the most difficult position for a rookie to play, and very few are ever given the opportunity to try. John Mackovic, the coach of the Kansas City Chiefs, described some of the difficulties. "On first and ten it won't be hard for him to read the coverages. But when he gets to second and long, there'll be a nickel defense put in all of a sudden. And the *next* second and long, when he's looking for it again—all of a sudden it *won't* be there. Then on third down he'll suddenly see a nickel with all its possible variations—and suddenly there'll be a blitz."

The tough task was made that much more difficult because Coach Reeves used the complicated Dallas Cowboys multiple-set offense that he had learned over fourteen years as a player and coach under Tom Landry. And the Broncos didn't have a strong supporting cast. They were a young team coming off a losing season. With super hype John had been built up to be Superman. But John wasn't Superman, and hype can't read a defense or pick up a blitz. Before John had taken his first regular-season snap, the smooth glide of the California coast had been transformed into the rough road of the Colorado Rockies.

John's first regular-season action came against the Steelers in Pittsburgh. The Steelers gave John a rough initiation as they sacked him four times, intercepted him once, and finally knocked him out of the game with a bruised elbow after he had completed only one pass in eight attempts.

The next game was in Baltimore, and the 99-degree temperature matched the heat of the hostile crowd that had come to boo John. The boos were so loud that according to Reeves, "You couldn't hear anything in the stadium. He couldn't even call the plays in the huddle. I've never seen anybody treated like that. It was terrible."

The Colt players did their part by sacking John three times and holding him to only nine completions in 21 attempts before he was replaced by DeBerg.

John played a decent game in the home opener against the Eagles. He threw his first TD pass, a 33-yarder to Rick Parros that tied the game late in the fourth quarter. But the Broncos lost the game, and the 75,000 Broncomaniacs in Mile High Stadium showered John with boos. In just a few weeks John had gone from Superman to Clark Kent.

The situation deteriorated rapidly as the Raiders came to town and banged and battered John and knocked him out of the game with a concussion. The Bears were next, and they completely dominated Denver. John was blitzed ferociously and was held to 36 yards passing, and the entire offense produced only 36 yards and no points in the first half. In the second half John was on the bench, and that's where he would stay for the next four games.

Denver had lost three of its first five games, and the two victories had come when DeBerg came off the bench to rally a team that was averaging less than two touchdowns per game. Reeves decided that a change was necessary and announced that DeBerg would be the starter. "I guess I expected too much out of John," he said with obvious regret. After John found out that he was being benched, he was disappointed, but he was also relieved; he knew it was for the best. "It got me out of the fire for a while. It's a terrible feeling to drop back and not know what is going on in front of you, but that's how it goes for a rookie quarterback in this league.

"I was so confused, my mind was going a hundred miles a minute, and with all that static in my mind, I couldn't react. I worried about calling the formations and getting the play off without a delay-of-game penalty. I couldn't even *think* about the defense.

"All of a sudden there were no weaknesses. In college it's common for receivers to get a fifteen-yard cushion from defensive backs. But in the pros, unless the other team blows a coverage, nobody is going to be wide open." At the time of his benching, John had the lowest pass-efficiency rating (42.3) in the entire league. He had completed 38 passes in 83 attempts, and he had thrown five interceptions and only one TD pass, and had been sacked 15 times. The statistics were an accurate indication of John's confusion. He couldn't read where the rush would come from, and he didn't know where his receivers would be.

John had lost his confidence and the sheer joy of playing. A quarterback must be a leader, and you can't lead without confidence in your own abilities. "I'm not the same quarterback I was in college, when I had a familiar offense around me. If I got pressure in college, I stepped up in the pocket or moved out of it and knew where to find my receivers. And I'm definitely not having fun."

John was down for the first time in his life, but he was determined to get back up. "To me it's a challenge to be strong. I'm going to beat it. It's going to take time. It certainly wasn't today. Maybe it won't be next week or even this year. But eventually I'm going to get it."

One of the lowest points in a season of low points came two days after the Chicago game, when John and teammates Mark Cooper and Keith Uecker went up to Wyoming on a day off. "We're sitting in a little roadside restaurant, and this guy next to us is saying that Elway has lost every game for the Broncos. He didn't know who I was, so Keith finally said, 'If you're going to talk about a man, at least look him in the face.' Suddenly I realized that people on the outside thought it was all my fault. You can't blame *everything* on one guy, especially a rookie quarterback. That's when I knew that I would never be given the opportunity that every rookie gets—the opportunity to *be* a rookie and make mistakes."

DeBerg went on to lead Denver to four consecutive victories, but he went down with a shoulder injury in the tenth game. John was back in the fire, and he kept getting burned by blitzing linebackers and his own inexperience.

During an interview with WNBC sportscaster Len Berman, John was asked if he was a 5-million-dollar mistake. John was stunned. "I don't mind reporters asking tough questions—that's part of the job. But a five-million-dollar mistake? I said, 'I'm a rookie. I'm twenty-three years old. Maybe we should wait awhile before we pass judgment.' "

A building tension between a frustrated rookie and a disappointed coach finally erupted on the sidelines after John had blown a formation call and thrown an interception against San Diego in the thirteenth game of the season. "He came off the field, and I was about to say something," recalls Reeves. "And he snapped, 'I know, I know I missed it.' But I wanted him to stand there and listen. It was then that the confrontation occurred."

The sideline screaming match caused John's game and concentration to further deteriorate. It finally reached the point where he became so distracted that on one play he lined up to take the snap from guard Tom Glassic instead of center Bill Bryan. "He had his hands under me, and I was trying to kick his foot," Glassic said. "Billy and I were yelling, 'Wrong guy, wrong guy!' It was disastrous."

"My mind was all clogged up," remembers John. "Nothing I did seemed right. It was like a snowball, and it kept getting bigger." John Hadl, the Broncos' quarterback coach, knew as a former quarterback himself what it was like to be a rookie quarterback and to see the players move but not be able to decipher the patterns. "Things happen so fast out there, it's like a jailbreak. You're getting coached a lot. You have to learn the system and the way the coaches want it done. Then you start to think quite a bit, and sometimes you think too much. Then you go blank."

After the game Coach Reeves realized that he had to do something to change the atmosphere. He met with his rookie quarterback and made a pact. "I told him that I'd be more patient if he would. We both had to mature. I had to learn somethings as a coach, and he had to learn as a quarterback. He has so much talent that I expected him to go out and perform miracles. It was unfair on my part. I didn't know how much was involved in starting a rookie quarterback."

Around the league, though, fans were wondering why another

rookie quarterback, Dan Marino, who was only the 27th pick in the draft, was on his way to a Pro Bowl season. Reeves bristled at the comparisons. "Let's face it, Shula has more experience bringing along young quarterbacks than I have. He's been in the league twenty years. Plus, John stepped into a two and seven team. Marino has better players around him. They went to the Super Bowl last year without him."

John is too much of a competitor not to have been stung by the comparisons, but all he would say is, "I don't like to compare myself to anybody. The situations are totally different."

In the next two games John began to give some evidence of why he was the number one pick. He threw for 284 yards and two touchdowns in leading the Broncos past the Browns. And in the next game he threw for 348 yards and brought the Broncos back from a 19–0 deficit against Baltimore by throwing three fourth-quarter touchdown passes. The 21–19 victory over the Colts was especially sweet, since it clinched a play-off berth for Denver.

But John's inexperience and inconsistency returned in the next game, the final game of the regular season. John was as cold as the −30-degree wind chill registered at Arrowhead Stadium in Kansas City as he completed only 13 passes in 34 attempts while throwing four interceptions.

Reeves selected DeBerg to start the wild-card play-off game against Seattle, but neither Steve nor John was up to the task as the Seahawks beat the Broncos 31–7. The Seattle game was a disappointing end to a season that had begun with great, if unrealistic, expectations. John had shown flashes of brilliance, but the final statistics, which showed John at the bottom of the AFC rankings, painted an accurate picture of his season. He completed only 47.5% of his passes, and he threw twice as many interceptions (14) as touchdown passes. His season hadn't snapped, crackled, or popped; it had just turned to mush like a bowl of soggy cereal.

A few months after the season, after John put some distance between himself and the hurt and frustration, he sat down and expressed how he felt. "Last year was the worst, and the longer I played the worse it got. I remember after the Chicago game I wished I could jump five years into the future. Now at least the whole world knows I'm not Superman, like they said I was supposed to be.

"As much as I said that things didn't bother me, they did. There was too much early hype, too many interviews and picture sessions. It never stopped. Then the frustrations of failing and all the negative comments worked against me. I put too much pressure on myself. I began worrying about every play. I became my own worst enemy."

John had also been hurt by the constant booing of the Denver fans. "They turned on me, and I have to admit that now I feel a little cold towards them. The odd thing is they kept coming for autographs. I couldn't figure it out. I'd sign them and say, 'Why am I signing this? For throwing twice as many interceptions as touchdowns?' What's great, though, is that when I'm really feeling bad, I just call my dad. It's a great mental pickup. When I hang up, I'm sunshine." John determined to protect himself for the coming season by getting mentally tougher, growing a scar to cover the hurt. Or as John put it, "My skin is about three inches thick these days."

John hadn't been able to cope with the flood of information and the vise of pressure: too many reporters, too many new plays, and too much anxiety.

John's natural talent and football instincts had been locked in a frozen maze of formations and his own insecurities. He had been trying to soar like a bird without wings.

Coach Reeves had seen the exceptional talent and made the mistake of thinking that it would come to full flower without first being nurtured. "It was my fault," he acknowledged. "John's knowledge of the offense was memory, not understanding. He knew the code, but he didn't know what it meant. We were using a complex offense that John wasn't ready to handle. There is no question that if I had it to do over again I would not have started him. There was no way that I could prepare him for all the defenses they threw at him last year."

Reeves made two moves before the 1984 season began that would help John and get the offense untracked. He brought in Mike Shanahan as the team's offensive coordinator and he traded Steve DeBerg. "With Steve gone, it left no questions," said Reeves. "Everyone had to look to John." And John wouldn't have to look over his shoulder if he was having a tough day. It was his team.

John was, as usual, optimistic about the upcoming season. He had a year of experience under his belt, and he was excited about working with Coach Shanahan. "He's the best thing that's ever happened to me, quarterbackwise," said John. Shanahan simplified the offensive formations and play calling, and he worked on developing a stronger rushing game, which would keep the defenses honest and take the pressure off the passing game.

But when the season began, John sputtered. After connecting with Butch Johnson to give Denver its first points of the 1984 season, John went out with an injury that kept him out of the second half and all of the following game. Denver won their next five games, and John did show improvement over his rookie year, but the victories were more a result of the revitalized running game and a dominant defense.

In the eighth game, a 37–7 blowout of Buffalo, John started to show the first sure signs of stardom. In less than a half he directed Denver to 23 points, including two TD passes. A shoulder injury caused him to sit out the second half and the next game, too. But he bounced back from the injury and over the next five games demonstrated that the Bills' game hadn't been a fluke.

The first game in the streak was a thriller against Tony Eason and the New England Patriots. John heard the familiar sound of booing from Bronco fans early in the game as the Pats took the lead. But he had come into the game with a new determination.

"All the other games I was coming in with a defensive attitude, trying to keep myself from making mistakes. I decided to be myself, be aggressive."

John was devastating; he threw for 315 yards and three TD's, including one in the fourth quarter that tied the game and set up a Denver victory. He also began to provide the leadership that a quarterback must establish to gain the respect of his teammates and without which an offense can't function effectively. "John came into the huddle and was firing everyone up," said wide receiver Steve Watson. "John took absolute control."

The following week the Chargers were ahead 13–9 with only 3:13 left, but John drove Denver 77 yards in ten plays, and they punched across the winning TD with only 38 seconds left in the game. John took all the drama out of the next game, though, by throwing five touchdown passes in a 42–21 rout of the Vikings. After the game John was all smiles. "This is fun."

Seattle was next, and John was forced to play catch-up against the Seahawks. John tossed two touchdown passes and set up a third score with a 63-yard toss. But with just over two minutes left to play, Denver still trailed 27–24. John engineered a drive down to the eight-yard line to set up an easy field goal that would have sent the game into overtime. But Rich Karlis's kick hit the upright, and Denver's ten-game winning streak was history. But John's streak wasn't over. In an instant replay of the preceding week, John led Denver into easy field-goal range against Kansas City. But Karlis again hit the upright, and the Broncos lost. The following week against San Diego, John rallied Denver for the third consecutive time, and this time Karlis nailed the winning field goal to give the Broncos a 16–13 win.

The five-game streak served as a reminder of John's promise and a preview of his greatness. He had shown the NFL and the Broncomaniacs in Denver that he could put points on the board in bunches, and he had also shown that he had the rare talent, like a magician who pulls rabbits out of a hat, of pulling victories out of defeats.

Denver closed out the regular season with a 31–14 victory over Seattle to clinch the AFC Western Division Championship. During the game John gave ample evidence of his abundant talent as well as the inconsistency that often comes with inexperience. He scored the first TD himself on a short run, which he set up with a 73-yard pass completion on the third play of the game. Later he threw for a score, and he kept the Seahawks' defense off balance throughout the game by scrambling nine times for 43 yards. But he also gave the Seattle offense plenty of opportunities, by throwing four interceptions.

In his first AFC play-off game, John displayed the same inconsistencies that he had against the Seahawks, but this time with different results. He opened the scoring against the Steelers with a short pass and gave Denver a 17–10 lead with a third-period strike to Steve Watson. But in the fourth period John had a pass picked off and returned to Denver's two-yard line with only 2:45 left. Two plays later Frank Pollard punched across the goal line to give Pittsburgh a 24–17 lead. Denver had two more possessions, but John had run out of magic and last-minute miracles.

The season had ended on a disappointing note, but John had taken great strides. The thirteen victories in the regular season were the most ever for a Denver team, and although he was only the eighth-ranked quarterback in the AFC, he had begun to show why he had been targeted for greatness. He had not only raised his game several notches above where it had been in his rookie year, but he had also demonstrated a unique ability to raise the level of his play—and the play of his teammates—when a game was on the line. As Steve Watson said, ''John takes the game to the limit.'' There is an all-news radio station in New York City that has a slogan, ''Give us twenty-two minutes, and we'll give you the world.'' If John had a slogan, it could be, ''Give me two minutes, and I'll give you the game.''

After the 1983 season John had left town, wanting to forget a sour season. But in 1984 John had decided to put down roots in the Denver area. He also began to work out with weights during the off-season at the suggestion of his boyhood idol, Roger Staubach. John had added new muscle to his 6'3" frame and looked like he could play tight end. According to Mike Shanahan, "John did more work from the end of football season than anyone in the league. He is very serious about wanting to be the best."

Shanahan had also altered the offense so that receivers would run "reaction" routes. Simply put, instead of running precise, predetermined patterns, receivers could change a pattern based upon how the defensive backs reacted to their moves. This approach would allow John, according to Shanahan, "to do what he does best—just drop back and throw." It would allow the Bronco offense to take advantage of the strongest arm in football. John's arm is so strong, in fact, that after a game you can see the impression that the point of the football has left on a receiver's chest. Since his days at Stanford, receivers have worn the "Elway cross" as a badge of honor.

John had a simple explanation for why he had worked so hard. "I hate to fail. My rookie year was the first time I'd ever been faced with something where nothing came easy. In college I could make up for my lack of understanding through my ability to play. In the NFL you can't do that. Last year the confidence started coming back. I *knew* what was going on. This year I have a point to prove—that John Elway is the quarterback everyone thought I could be."

According to Cincinnati Coach Sam Wyche, everyone else in the NFL was thinking the same thing. "Nobody plays Denver without worrying if that could be the game Elway explodes. John is a time bomb waiting to go off."

John started the season strongly by tossing two TD passes against the Rams. And in the next two games, with victories over New Orleans and Atlanta, John soared with the eagles. He completed 45 passes in 78 attempts, good for 644 yards and seven TD tosses. John was flying high as Dan Marino and the Dolphins flew into Denver.

The stage was set for a classic confrontation as a national TV audience joined a capacity crowd at Mile High Stadium to watch the first duel between John and Dapper Dan. The matchup proved to be no contest, though, as Marino threw for 390 yards and three TD's while leading the Dolphins to a 30–26 victory. John's numbers read: 250 yards, no TD's, and a critical interception that ended Denver's last threat. It was a disappointing performance for John.

With the exception of one patch of four games when John hit the skids and didn't throw a single touchdown pass, his play was a model of inconsistency. He continued to show flashes of total brilliance and absolutely frustrated his opponents. As Raider linebacker Matt Millen said, "You spend all week studying films, preparing for guys to run certain routes, then all of a sudden he's out of the pocket and there are no routes anymore. It's inevitable somebody is going to get open." But John also hit lots of low notes. His inconsistency was obvious in the last two games of the season. He threw five interceptions against the Chiefs and the following week threw for 432 yards against the Seahawks, the second-highest total in the AFC in 1985.

The season ended disappointingly as Denver failed to make the play-offs despite an 11–5 record that was better than half of the teams that did make them. And while John had thrown for more yardage than anyone except Marino and had led the league in total offense, after three full seasons he still hadn't delivered on his extraordinary promise of unlimited potential.

3

Sweet Smell of Success

In 1986 John was determined to finally answer the question "Whatever happened to John Elway?" This was going to be the season that his accomplishments would match his abilities.

John didn't waste any time in proving the point. In the first game of the season, on their very first possession, John led the Broncos on a lightning-quick, four-play, 70-yard drive that he finished off with a 35-yard TD toss to Steve Watson. John scored Denver's next TD and set a record when he *caught* a 23-yard pass on a trick play from halfback Steve Sewell. It was the longest pass reception for a touchdown by a full-time quarterback in NFL history. In the fourth quarter John threw his second TD pass to give the Broncos a thrilling 38–36 win over the Raiders.

John continued his sharpshooting the following week with three TD passes against the Steelers. Two weeks later, after he had brought Denver back to beat New England, Andre Tippett, the Patriots' all-pro linebacker, was asked to compare John to other NFL quarterbacks. "Elway," he replied, "is one of a kind."

By the end of the regular season Tippett's opinion had gained league-wide acceptance, and John had been selected to appear in the Pro Bowl. He had finished the season with more than 3,000 yards passing for the second consecutive year and had led all AFC quarterbacks in rushing for the third consecutive year. John had also led Denver to an 11–5 record and the championship of the AFC Western Division.

In the play-offs John led the Broncos to their first postseason victory since 1977 by directing them to a 22–17 win over New England. John registered the first score on a 22-yard scamper and then put the winning points on the board with a 48-yard scoring strike to speedster Vance Johnson. Then it was on to Cleveland to play the Browns for the AFC Championship.

There are certain performances that occur in championship contests that are so charged with drama and greatness that they leave an indelible memory in people's consciousness and become a part of our folklore. Baseball fans still remember Bobby Thompson's home run against Ralph Branca in the top of the ninth inning that won the 1951 pennant for the New York Giants. Sports fans around the world still recall the astonishing victories of the United States hockey team at Lake Placid in the 1980 Winter Olympics. Football fans still talk excitedly about the NFL's first overtime game, the 1958 clash between the Colts and the Giants, a game that many fans still claim to be the greatest ever played. And just mention Doug Flutie's name, and everyone remembers The Pass against the University of Miami. The 1986 championship game between the Broncos and the Browns has, like those other great contests, become a part of the mythology of sports.

The game began unspectacularly and quickly settled into an uneventful, mistake-filled contest. It was almost as though the arctic air that lashed Memorial Stadium and froze the field had also frozen the talents of the players. The Browns scored first, when quarterback Bernie Kosar capped a long drive with a six-yard pass, and Denver scored its TD on a short run after John had set it up by scrambling for 34 yards. In the middle of the fourth quarter Denver led 13–10 as neither team was able to mount an effective offense. And then, with less than six minutes left to play and with the sudden and unpredictable swiftness of a tornado, the game changed utterly.

Cleveland had the ball on a third and six just inside Denver territory. Kosar took the snap, faded back, saw Brian Brennan streaking for the end zone, and delivered a 48-yard TD pass to give Cleveland a 20–13 lead with 5:43 left to play. The Cleveland fans erupted, visions of a Super Bowl trip filling their thoughts.

The Broncos mishandled the kickoff, and when they finally

downed the ball, it was on their own two-yard line. When John trotted onto the field, there was only 5:34 left to play, and the Cleveland goal line was 98 yards away. Up until this point John had been virtually stymied. He had been held to only 14 completions in 26 attempts for 116 yards. There was too little time and too many yards to go; it was the impossible dream. But John entered the huddle with a smile on his face. "It was a cocky smile," said Steve Watson. "He told us, 'If you work hard, good things will happen.' And then he smiled again. I figured, 'Shoot, if he was going to be that loose, let's go for it.'"

John got some breathing room with a five-yard completion, and four plays later, chased from the pocket, he scrambled 11 yards for a first down. With the clock winding down to the two-minute warning, John rifled a 22-yarder to Sewell and a 12-yarder to Watson to put the ball in Cleveland territory at the 40-yard line. After the time-out John threw an incompletion and on second down was sacked for an eight-yard loss. John was in the shotgun on a third and 18, and as Watson went in motion behind the line, the center snapped the ball, glancing it off Watson's leg. John reacted instinctively, plucked the ball off his shoe tops, and fired a 20-yard completion to Mark Jackson at the 28. The fans at the open end of the stadium were throwing dog biscuits and barking for their Dawgs to play d-e-f-e-n-s-e. John threw an incompletion and then connected with Sewell for 14. After another incompletion John was chased out of the pocket, but he escaped the rush and scrambled nine yards down to the five-yard line with 42 seconds left. On the next play John hit Jackson for the TD, and the extra point tied the game with only 37 seconds showing on the clock. John had finally put it all together: the talent, the leadership, and the poise under pressure, and he had done it on a national stage, in a championship game. And in the process he had put together the most dramatic drive in play-off history. It would, in fact, forevermore be known as The Drive.

The Browns won the coin toss in the overtime session, but still stunned by John's last minute heroics, they only ran three quick plays and punted. Defensive back Felix Wright summed up their feelings. "We were trying to get each other up, but it hurts when you're ahead like that and let it get away. It affects you."

Denver took over on its own 25-yard line, and still pumped up from The Drive, rode John's strong right arm down the field. He hit Orson Mobley for 22 yards, and then, on a third and 12, John ran out of the pocket, froze the Cleveland secondary, and hummed a 28-yard rope to Steve Watson down to the Cleveland 22. Three running plays moved the ball to the 15-yard line, and as Karlis came in to attempt the winning field goal, John went by and yelled, "Just like practice, just like practice." It was just what Rich needed to settle down, and he calmly put the ball through the uprights for the 23–20 overtime victory.

After the game Coach Reeves was asked whether he thought Denver had a chance after Cleveland had taken the lead. "Whenever you have John Elway as your quarterback," he replied, "you always have a chance." A lot of John's teammates seemed as happy for him personally as they were about being in the Super Bowl. They had resented all the criticism that John had taken throughout the years and felt it had been unjustified. "John showed a lot of people today," said Steve Watson. "First the Pro Bowl and now the Super Bowl."

The Giants were heavy favorites to win Super Bowl XXI. They had gone 14–2 during the regular season, closing with nine consecutive victories. In the play-offs they had demolished the 49ers 49–3 and whitewashed Washington 17–0. They had one of the best defenses ever assembled, anchored by Lawrence Taylor, the NFL's MVP, and Carl Banks. And they had a strong offense that featured the running of Joe Morris, the passing of Phil Simms, and the receiving and blocking of tight end Mark Bavaro.

Almost all the experts agreed that the Giants had the better team, but Denver had John Elway, and that caused most of the experts to hedge their opinions. Steve Ortmeyer, the director of football operations for the Los Angeles Raiders, summed up their thoughts. "The Giants have a better team, no doubt about it. But the biggest factor for Denver is their quarterback. Elway thrives on big games. The bigger they are, the more fun he has. That's why I think Denver is in it.''

The Giant players also had it scoped. "The biggest thing we have to do,'' said all-pro Lawrence Taylor, "is to stop John Elway.'' Added safety Kenny Hill, "He makes great plays out of lost plays.'' And Coach Bill Parcells voiced his concern and admiration. "Elway is one player you have to keep in mind on every play. And he's a fighter. He gets hit, he gets knocked out of the game, and he comes back.''

John threw the Giants off balance on the very first play from scrimmage. He faked a handoff to the right, spun around, and raced left for a first down. He rattled the Giants by completing his first six passes and eight of his first ten, to give Denver a 10–9 halftime lead. The Broncos had missed an opportunity to take command of the game by failing to score on three consecutive running plays after John had led them to the Giants' one-yard line. The failure was magnified by the fact that they came away completely empty when Karlis missed the easy field goal.

In the second half the superiority of the Giants began to assert itself. Their defense dominated Denver's porous offensive line and didn't give John any room to operate. Phil Simms, playing the best game of his career, sparked the offense, and the Giants won 39–20.

But even in defeat John had shown his greatness. Against a great defense that was designed to stop him, he still passed for over 300 yards and one touchdown. He was also Denver's leading rusher and scored a touchdown himself. No one was asking where John Elway was. He was right there at the top of the stack.

It had been a long and difficult climb, but John had reached the top and liked the view. He was determined to stay there, to improve even, and to get Denver back into the Super Bowl.

He opened the 1987 season with an explosive performance against Seattle, the team that ranked number one in points defense in the AFC in 1986, throwing four TD passes while completing 22 of 32 for 338 yards. The 504 yards of total offense were the most that the Broncos had accumulated since John had come to Denver.

But the Broncos lost their next game, and then the players' strike disrupted the season. When the regulars returned, their performance was lackluster. After eight games they had a 4–3–1 record, with a game coming up against the Bears. They were in real danger of not making the play-offs.

"We were playing like we didn't care," observed John. "We were playing like we didn't want to be out there, like the game wasn't fun. There didn't seem to be any commitment or enjoyment."

So John decided to take charge and called a players' meeting. "I told them we were too talented to be playing that badly. I told them that we were lucky to be playing pro football and that our careers are too short to waste a year. Let's have some fun and win some games, I told them. I really feel that way."

John's words inspired his teammates, and that same week Coach Reeves decided to use the shotgun as their primary formation, to fully take advantage of John's talents. The inspiration and the strategy paid off as John threw three TD passes to lead Denver to a thrilling 31–29 come-from-behind victory over Chicago. The Broncos went on to win five of their last six games and win the AFC Western Division title with a 10–4–1 record.

Greg Townsend, a defensive end for the Raiders, expressed the frustration of all of Denver's opponents. "Elway can do so much out of the shotgun. He can run with it, and that's a threat. He can give it to somebody and they can run with it, and that's a threat. And he can throw that sucker like nobody else. That's the *worst* threat."

Despite missing four games because of the strike, John threw for more than 3,000 yards for the third straight season, rushed for 304 yards, the most in his career and enough to lead all AFC quarterbacks for the fourth consecutive season, and scored four touchdowns. John's play and leadership qualities had grown tremendously, and his efforts were rewarded when he was selected as the starting quarterback for the AFC in the Pro Bowl and the NFL's MVP by the Associated Press.

In an AFC divisional play-off game John led Denver to a 34–10 humbling of Houston by throwing for two scores and running for a third. Then it was time for instant replay against Cleveland as John Elway and the Denver Broncos hooked up with Bernie Kosar and the Cleveland Browns for the AFC championship.

Denver looked like it was going to run away with the game as Bernie couldn't get Cleveland's offense in gear while John drove Denver to a 21–3 halftime lead. But the Broncos knew that the lead wasn't secure. As wide receiver Ricky Nattiel put it, "I knew that pretty soon they'd start *bringing* it."

Kosar began to bring it as Cleveland scored the first four times they had the ball in the second half, and near the end of the fourth quarter he had thrown three TD passes and Cleveland had tied the score 31–31. The game was unraveling for Denver, and as they put the ball in play at their 25-yard line, John was concerned. "We knew we had to score there. And with Bernie being so hot, we knew that three points wasn't going to be enough."

John, operating out of the shotgun, hit Ricky Nattiel for 26 yards on first down. Three plays later, on third and seven, he hit Nattiel, again for 26, down to the Cleveland 20. On first down John dropped back, drew the pass rush to him, and then lofted a perfect screen pass over the middle to running back Sammy Winder. Winder took it in for the score, and the Broncos led 38–31. If they had been filming a movie, they could have called it *The Drive, Part Two*. Kosar, though, wasn't finished. With 3:53 left, he began a drive that had the Browns at Denver's goal line, but just as Earnest Byner was taking the ball in to tie the score, Jeremiah Castille stripped the ball out of his hands and then recovered the fumble.

Denver had held on, but just barely. As John said afterward, "This game scared me to death. Even with seven seconds left I was scared to death. The Browns would never quit. We couldn't shake them. It was a great, great game." And John and Bernie had put on another great, great show, combining for 637 yards passing and six touchdown passes. They had turned in another classic that could be put in a time capsule.

The evaluation of John throughout the league was virtually unanimous. John had crossed the threshold from merely having great talent to being a great player—and the best quarterback in the NFL. It was that greatness that caused most football experts to pick Denver to win Super Bowl XXII, even though they thought that Washington had bigger, better, and stronger players.

Tom Landry, the longtime Dallas coach, spoke for a lot of people when he said, "I believe that John Elway's unique ability to make the big play gives the Broncos a slight edge. Elway, in my opinion, is the top quarterback in the league. Better than Montana, Marino, or Kosar. Elway has it all, including the magic of the great quarterbacks who can win in the last two minutes. John Elway can *singlehandedly* ruin an opponent."

John and Coach Reeves both scoffed at the notion that Denver was a one-man team. "I must have answered that question a thousand times," John said with some heat at a pre-Super Bowl press conference. "Everyone knows it's not a one-man team. If you're not coordinated as a team, you're not going to be successful."

Reeves tried to make a joke of the question when he was asked about a curfew. "Well, since we're a one-man team, only one guy has a curfew. Number seven has a curfew. The other forty-four guys can do what they want to do."

John's talent had begun to be viewed as such a dominant factor that Bob Hollway, the director of pro personnel for the Vikings, gave this assessment. "John Elway is the best all-around quarterback I've ever seen. The only way that they can stop him is to keep him on the sidelines with long drives. That's the only way I can see Washington winning. If Elway is given enough chances, he'll figure out a way to win the game." And Hollway said this despite the fact that the Vikings had beaten Denver during the season and had lost *twice* to Washington.

Ralph Hawkins, the defensive coordinator of the Seahawks, may have paid John the ultimate compliment when he observed, "Elway's developed to the point where he's like Larry Bird or Wayne Gretzky. He makes his teammates better because of his unique skills." And two of those teammates, Vance Johnson and Mark Jackson, two of the trio of celebrated receivers known as the Three Amigos, confirmed Hawkins's observation.

"He's a great player and a great leader," said Johnson. "Without John, the Broncos would be home watching MTV."

"Elway's the MVP of the league," noted Jackson, "but on our team he's more than the MVP. We've built our team around him. We go as Elway goes."

For the first quarter of the Super Bowl, it looked as if they'd go all the way. Throwing from the shotgun on first down, Elway hit Ricky Nattiel for a 56-yard touchdown, and the Broncos were up 7-0 and in the record book for the fastest TD in Super Bowl history. Later in the quarter Rich Karlis kicked a field goal to give Denver a 10-0 lead and a look of invincibility.

But then the most sudden reversal in Super Bowl history took place in the second quarter, and Denver's dream turned into a nightmare. In 13 minutes and 13 seconds of the second quarter, Washington scored touchdowns on five consecutive possessions and took a commanding 35-10 lead.

Washington, though, wasn't celebrating prematurely. In the locker room defensive coordinator Richie Petitbon reminded his team, "Elway can kill you if you give him a chance." But there was no magic comeback as Washington's defense continued their domination in the second half and the offense added a final TD, almost as an exclamation point, to make the final score 42-10.

Afterward, Dave Butz, Washington's mammoth defensive tackle, summed up what a lot of his teammates were feeling. "What makes it even more meaningful," he said, referring to John, "was that we beat the best there was."

After the game John refused to alibi or blame the defense. "The offense shares in the fault. When they got moving, we had to do something to take the momentum away. If they score fifty, our job is to score fifty-one.''

Despite the two consecutive Super Bowl losses, John has established himself as one of the all-time great quarterbacks. And as one defensive coordinator said with amazement, ''He just keeps improving.'' In the last four years he has had more wins than any quarterback in the NFL.

John has come a long way in other respects too. He has grown more confident and self-assured. ''Once I started to realize that I don't have to live up to other people's expectations, I started to play better football.''

What's special about John is that, despite the constant pressure for his time, he still takes the time to talk to reporters and sign autograph books. And John hasn't let the fame or the money go to his head. ''I look at life like I did when I was in the seventh or eighth grade. I'm playing a game that's fun, and I want to win. So you know, I'm still the same guy I was when I walked in here. And I'll still be the same when I walk out.''

John Elway looking good for the Oneonta Yankees.

John checks out the situation, waiting for a Stanford receiver to get loose.

John scrambles away from the rush.

(Rod Hanna. Courtesy of the Denver Broncos.)

John smokes one for 6 points.

John sets up against Cleveland in the 1987 AFC Championship game.

John looking for help against Washington, but not finding it.

Bernie Kosar passing the University of Miami to victory over Nebraska in the Orange Bowl.

(Caryn Levy. Courtesy of the University of Miami.)

Bernie gets a little help from his friends as he sets up to throw.

Bernie draws a crowd as he gets set to hand-off against Washington.

(John Reid. Courtesy of the Cleveland Browns.)

In the 1987 AFC Championship game against Denver, Bernie takes the snap . . .

Drops back and checks the defense . . .

Then lets it fly.

(Mitchell B. Reibel, SportsChrome.)

BERNIE KOSAR

1

Hometown Boy

Bernard J. Kosar, Jr., was born November 25, 1963. He grew up about sixty miles from Cleveland, in Boardman, Ohio, a suburb of Youngstown.

Bernie was raised in a very close-knit family, which included his mother and father, his sister Beth, and his younger brother Brian.

Bernie senior always made it easy for Bernie to play ball around the yard, but he wouldn't let him play organized football until the seventh grade. "It was ridiculous," he thought, "for kids to be placed in such a rigid structure at such a young age. Even if they don't get hurt, they can get burned out."

Bernie's dad liked sports, but he didn't push Bernie into participating in athletics. His philosophy about playing ball was, "If it feels good, do it; and if it doesn't, then don't do it."

What Bernie senior did push, however, was the pursuit of other interests and schoolwork. He would always tell Bernie to reach a little farther. "All the time Bernie was in school, if he was taking four courses I would ask him to take five. I told him, 'All I'm asking is that you do just twenty percent more than you are doing.' "

Bernie's drive to succeed and his thirst for knowledge revealed itself at an early age. As his mother, who is a registered nurse, tells the story, "After his second day in the first grade, Bernie ran home and announced that he wasn't going back. 'They still haven't taught me how to read,' he said with a pout." As he got older, Bernie's mom would frequently find him at the breakfast table at six A.M., studying before he left for school.

Bernie senior also helped to instill a sense of self-confidence.

He told Bernie, "Don't be afraid to fail. History," he explained, "is made by people who get up one more time than they get knocked down."

He emphasized that success in anything in life stems from two qualities: concentration and self-discipline. You have to use the powers of your mind, and you have to be motivated enough to move *yourself* toward your goal. Bernie senior knew that the push had to come from within each person. If you want to succeed, you have to read that next chapter, or throw that next pass, or strive for whatever your goal is, even when you're tired or when the TV set seems to be calling to you.

If you concentrate and practice self-discipline, he knew, you would start to move toward your goal. That movement would create confidence, and then that confidence would help you take the next step.

Bernie put his dad's advice to good use and went on to achieve great accomplishments.

Bernie was an outstanding athlete at Boardman High School. He played varsity baseball for three years, and in his senior year he batted .347 (third highest on the team) as a third baseman. He pitched a little too, and had a team-leading 2.40 ERA. He was also the co-captain of the basketball team and its leading scorer (232 points) and rebounder (182) during his senior year. (The team, which finished with an 8–13 record, obviously could have used even more help.)

It was on the football field, though, that Bernie's talent really shined. In his junior year he led the team to a 6–0 record (the season was shortened by a teachers' strike) while throwing for 680 yards. In his senior year he led the Spartans to an 8–2 mark while setting conference passing records by throwing for 2,222 yards and 19 touchdowns; he also ran for six TD's.

The Spartans' head coach, Gene Pushic, had this to say about Bernie's contributions. "His offensive play calling, reading of defenses, and execution of assignments were nearly flawless. It was almost like having an extra coach in the huddle. He had remarkable maneuverability both in the pocket and on the run. He picked up key first downs against teams that underestimated his running ability.''

Bernie's efforts were rewarded with many awards, including being named the quarterback on the all-state team and the Ohio Back of the Year by the AP.

He was also a very good student, whose efforts produced a 3.6 grade-point average (out of a possible 4.0) and a ranking of 50th out of a graduating class of 486.

Despite his athletic and academic accomplishments, Bernie wasn't very heavily recruited by colleges. He was totally ignored by one nearby college football power, the University of Pittsburgh (where Dan Marino had filled the air with footballs before taking his aerial act to the Miami Dolphins).

A lot of college coaches were concerned about his awkward throwing style and lack of speed. ''Coaches,'' Bernie notes, ''have been worrying about my speed and throwing style since seventh grade.''

Howard Schnellenberger, who was the head coach at the University of Miami, wasn't worried; he saw the picture differently. ''We recognized that he didn't have the prettiest arm action, but the *results* were always the best.'' Schnellenberger is not just another run-of-the-mill head coach; he is a superior coach who is especially good at devising offensive strategies and developing young quarterbacks. Earlier in his career he had been the offensive coordinator at the University of Alabama, where he helped develop Joe Namath and Kenny ''Snake'' Stabler, two all-time great quarterbacks.

The coach sensed something special about Bernie. ''After we spent some time learning about his character and his intelligence, it was obvious that he had some things that most kids don't have, and it was obvious that he was a *winner*.''

He might have been a winner, but he was still a youngster and

Miami had a lot of quarterback talent. Jim Kelly, who went on to the Buffalo Bills after dominating the USFL with the Houston Gamblers, was the senior and starter. Also in front of Bernie were Kyle Vanderwende and another freshman, Vinny Testaverde. As a senior, Vinny would win the Heisman Trophy as the best college football player in the country, and he became the number one pick in the 1987 NFL draft. The coaching staff decided to "redshirt" Bernie because he wasn't as physically developed as the players he would be competing against. Redshirting allows a player to attend classes and to work out and practice, but he doesn't get to play, so he doesn't lose one of his four years of athletic eligibility.

Bernie didn't complain or sit and pout. He worked hard in the classroom and on his football development. He studied the playbook, and he learned all that he could from assistant coaches Earl Morrall, who had been a quarterback in the NFL for twenty-one seasons, and Marc Trestman. Between them they taught Bernie how to run the complicated, pro-type attack that the Miami Hurricanes used. Trestman marveled at Bernie's ability to grasp the complexities of a sophisticated football system. "He's just smarter than anyone else, that's all."

"I knew," Bernie remembers, "if I was going to progress, I would have to be on top of the game mentally and have discipline. As far back as I can remember, my father was always telling me about concentration and self-discipline."

After the 1982 season, Bernie came to spring practice as the third-string quarterback. "I realized," Bernie says, "that it was the pivotal point in my career. I realized that whoever won the job would probably have it from then on. That was the most intense period of my life. I went into that situation in third place. I had to play better to win the job."

Coach Schnellenberger remembers that situation as "the best competition I've ever been around." As the coach tells it, "I was still wrestling with the decision five minutes before I was supposed to make the announcement. Our first game was against Florida, and I thought that we had better than a fifty-fifty chance to lose the game. I had to decide which quarterback would best be able to handle the loss and come back to play again.''

The coach finally made his decision. Bernie Kosar was selected to open the 1983 season as the starting quarterback. ''Another reason for selecting him over some kids who were better athletes was his ability to understand and run the offense—to get us in the right play at the line of scrimmage, to check off after reading the defense.''

Schnellenberger's concern about the game was well founded. Miami was demolished 28–3 by Florida. But Bernie wasn't demolished. He hung in and hit for 25 completions, tying Miami's single-game completion mark, set many years earlier by George Mira, a former all-American.

What impressed Coach Schnellenberger most about Bernie in that game, however, was not his passing but his poise. ''It's easy to stay cool when you win. It's tougher when you're getting your rear end kicked in front of 74,000 fanatic fans. We came out of that game a lot more confident than we went in.''

Bernie had survived the loss, and now he was ready to lead the Hurricanes on the wildest and highest ride in the history of the school.

After that season-opening loss the Hurricanes began to howl. Behind Bernie's pinpoint passing and a dominating defense, the victories began to mount up. After nine games the 'Canes were 8–1 with two games left on their schedule. They had moved up in the national rankings, and their faithful fans began to talk about the possibility of being invited to a postseason bowl game.

Then the sunny sky in Miami turned cloudy—Bernie had a sore and swollen ankle. Some people tried to joke about it. ''It won't matter, since Bernie can't run anyway.'' But no one in Miami laughed when the clock ticked down in the fourth quarter with the 'Canes trailing East Carolina. There were just a few minutes left, and the ball was 80 yards away from the goal line. Bernie trotted into the huddle, clapped his hands together, and said, ''Let's go get it.''

The team responded with a drive down the field, and with just 1:04 remaining, Bernie plunged the final yard into the end zone as Miami narrowly escaped with a 12–7 victory.

The last game of the regular season was against an archrival, Florida State. Bernie still had the ankle injury, and once again the 'Canes were trailing late in the game. They narrowed the gap to 16–14 when Bernie threw a 37-yard TD toss. But time was about to run out, though, as Miami got the ball back for one last possession. But once again they beat the clock as Bernie passed them into position for a game-winning 19-yard field goal on the *last* play of the game.

In his first season Bernie had led Miami to a 10–1 record, their best record since their initial season in 1926. The ten victories were the most ever for Miami, and their national rankings (number five by the AP's poll of writers, and number four by the UPI's poll of coaches) were their highest ever. It had been a sensational season for Bernie and the rest of the Hurricanes, but the best was yet to come! Miami was picked to play Nebraska in the 50th-anniversary edition of the Orange Bowl. It was the 'Canes' first invitation to a major bowl game since the 1951 team had played and lost to Clemson in the Orange Bowl.

The Nebraska Cornhuskers are a perennial power in college football, and they routinely get to play in major bowl games. This, in fact, was Nebraska's tenth appearance in the Orange Bowl classic, which takes its name from the stadium in which it is played (which also happens to be the home field of the University of Miami).

The Cornhuskers came into the contest with a twenty-two-game winning streak and the number one ranking in the country. They had a fine defense that had allowed an average of only 15.5 points per game and an offensive unit that was considered by many experts to be one of the strongest in the *entire* history of college football. They had *averaged* a phenomenal 52 points and 547 yards of total offense per game. The all-senior backfield included running back Mike Rozier, the 1983 Heisman Trophy award winner. Mike, who currently plays for the Houston Oilers, had rushed for 2,148 yards (only the second college player to ever rush for more than 2,000 yards) and scored 29 touchdowns, to tie the NCAA record for touchdowns in a regular season. Irving Fryar, who is currently a wide receiver for the New England Patriots, was the wingback; and the quarterback was Turner Gill, whose record as a college quarterback was 29–1.

Before the game began, most experts considered it to be a mismatch. The tough Miami defense might be able to dampen the explosive Nebraska attack, but the 'Canes' offense, it was thought, wouldn't be able to dent the defense of the Cornhuskers.

But once the game began, Bernie burst upon the scene like a Fourth of July fireworks display. He ignited the Miami offense and led the Hurricanes on scoring drives on their first three possessions. He finished the first drive with a two-yard toss to Glenn Dennison, and after setting up a 45-yard field goal, he connected with Dennison again, this time on a 22-yarder. After only fourteen minutes of play, the Hurricanes led 17–0 and had blown away mighty Nebraska's aura of invincibility. The fans on the Miami side of the Orange Bowl were whooping it up while the numbed Nebraska rooters sat in stunned silence.

The Cornhuskers began to bounce back in the second quarter after tackle Dean Steinkuhler scored a TD on a trick play. They added another score before halftime and then tied the game on a third-quarter field goal. But Bernie just fired the fuse again, cranked up his right arm, and led Miami to two more touchdowns and a 31–17 lead.

Nebraska, though, was not about to quit. They narrowed the lead to 31–24 on a one-yard, fourth-quarter run by Jeff Smith, and then, with only 48 seconds left in the game, Smith scored again to make the score 31–30.

Nebraska had the choice of going for an almost automatic extra point to gain a tie, which would preserve their unbeaten streak, or of going for the win with a tough two-point conversion try. Tom Osborne, the Nebraska coach, didn't hesitate; the Cornhuskers went for the victory. Gill aimed a pass at Smith in the end zone, but Ken Calhoun, a Miami defensive back, reached over and tipped the ball away. The game was over and the joy flowed through Miami like fresh-squeezed orange juice.

A new star had burst upon the world of college football. Bernie had lit up the scoreboard while throwing for an Orange Bowl record 300 yards as he led the Miami Hurricanes to a stunning upset over the Nebraska Cornhuskers. What impressed both fans and experts was not simply Bernie's passing skills but the way that the young man had led his team and kept his cool. His efforts were rewarded with the victory and his selection as the Orange Bowl MVP.

After the game reporters wanted to know if the Miami team was as surprised as most people by the outcome. "I knew we'd beat Nebraska," Bernie answered. "We did exactly what we were supposed to do." He was asked if he was nervous when Nebraska went for the two-point conversion. "No, I wanted them to make it." He would have *preferred* it if Nebraska had scored the two points. "There was plenty of time for us to at least get into position for a field goal. We would have done it too, the way we were moving the ball. Forty-eight seconds was more than enough time. It would've been *fun*."

The coaches and sportswriters gave Miami a perfect ending to its Cinderella season by selecting the Hurricanes as the number one college football team in the country.

The Hurricanes had earned the number-one ranking for the 1983 season. But they must have felt a little bit like Rodney Dangerfield, because when the first rankings for the 1984 season were released—before a single game had been played—they had been replaced at the top by the Auburn Tigers. The voters must have looked at Miami's schedule, which called for them to play three of the best teams in the country within a twelve-day period.

The first of the three games was against Auburn, which was led by its all-American halfback, Bo Jackson. The Tigers kept their lead and their ranking until there were less than ten minutes left in

62

the game. Then Bernie led the Hurricanes down the field and positioned the field goal that allowed them to walk off the field with a 20–18 win.

Less than a week later the 'Canes traveled to Tampa to tackle arch rival Florida. The competition between these intrastate rivals is always fierce. Miami was trailing 20–19 with only 40 seconds left and the ball deep in its own territory at the 28-yard line. In only four plays Bernie marched the 'Canes 60 yards to the Florida 12-yard line. There were only five seconds left on the scoreboard clock as Jimmy Johnson, the new Miami head coach, called time out to send in the field-goal unit to win the game. As 74,000 frenzied Florida fans hooted, Bernie ran over to the sidelines and told Johnson that he wanted to go for the TD. Johnson hesitated but finally gave the okay, and then a national TV audience and a stunned crowd saw Bernie calmly flick a TD pass to all-American wide receiver Eddie Brown to give Miami a last-play, come-from-behind victory.

After the game Johnson was asked why he had listened to Bernie and hadn't gone with the obvious, safe call—a short-range field goal. "I saw the look in Bernie's eyes and decided to go for it."

"I'm glad he saw the look," Bernie told reporters, "because I really wanted to win the game with what we do best. It wasn't a gutsy call," said the confident quarterback. "It's a safe and easy pattern as long as I know what I'm doing." He had shown that he knew what he was doing and that he had the courage to act out his convictions.

In their next game nothing seemed safe as Miami lost to a tough Michigan team, and Bernie suffered through the worst game of his college career. He was sacked three times, threw six interceptions, and, for the only time that season, completed less than fifty percent of his passes. "One reason I came to Miami was to play against all the best schools. I just didn't expect to play all of them in twelve days," he said with a smile.

"After games like these, I take a crash course to understand what went right or wrong. Then I go on to what's ahead."

As offensive tackle Paul Berticelli put it, "You can't get him to rehash a game unless you do it right afterward. He's always looking ahead to something else."

The last game on Miami's 1984 schedule was against Boston College. And it will always be remembered—by the people at the game and by the tens of millions of people who watched it on live TV or afterward on videotape replay—as perhaps the most memorable college football game ever played. In the wind and rain of a gray Miami afternoon Doug Flutie and Bernie Kosar put on one of the great offensive shows of all time.

Boston College took the initiative and jumped out to a 14–0 lead as Flutie hit on his first 11 passes. Bernie answered the bell and quickly came back with 11 consecutive completions of his own as the 'Canes tied the game at 14–14. By halftime BC had reclaimed the lead 28–21, and no one was leaving the stadium or turning any TV channels.

The teams were scoring points faster than a Roger Clemens fastball, and with less than three minutes left to play, BC was leading 41–38. The 'Canes were backed up deep in their own end, facing a third down with 21 yards to go for a first down. Bernie delivered a 20-yard strike, and they picked up the first down on the next play. Bernie and his teammates kept driving, grinding out the yardage on the slick field as the clock wound down. With less than a minute left in the game, Bernie handed off to his fullback, who plunged into the end zone to give Miami a 45–41 lead. The Orange Bowl rocked as the Miami fans showered their heroes, already celebrating on the sidelines, with cheers.

There were only 28 ticks left on the clock as Flutie took the snap at his own 20-yard line. A holding penalty and a pass completion moved the ball to the Miami 48-yard line. Then Doug threw an incomplete pass, and there were only six seconds left—time for one more play, one last desperate play. Flutie took the snap and began to backpedal as four wide receivers flashed toward the goal line. Flutie scrambled away from a tackle, and from his own 38-yard line, with one second left on the clock, threw the ball on a line toward the end zone, which was swarming with players from both teams. As Doug said after the game, "You throw and hope—it's a fifty-fifty chance your guy will come up with it." The odds are really much less than that, but this time his guy, wide receiver Gerald Phelan, came up with it, and Boston College had pulled out an amazing win, 47–45.

If you saw the game, you had the feeling that the Hurricanes hadn't really lost the game, they had just run out of time. Bernie had certainly done his part by throwing for two TD's and 447 yards, a single-game Miami record, but on this day he had to take a backseat to Doug Flutie and The Pass.

In only two years of quarterbacking the Hurricanes, Bernie had rewritten the Miami record book while leading them to a 19–5 record. In addition to setting four single-game records, he established nine single-season records and nine career records, including: most yards gained passing (5,971); most completed passes (463); most touchdown passes (40); and most 300-yard games passing (nine).

Bernie did more than compile fancy statistics—he won most of the tight games and most of the tough, high-pressure games. He was 5–1 versus teams that were ranked in the top ten, 2–0 versus teams who were ranked number one, and 6–2 in games in which Miami had appeared on national television. Bernie had measured up.

His former coach Howard Schnellenberger summed it all up. "He's a leader, always ready to seize the initiative. What sets him apart is that he expects himself to excel."

Hurricane fans were already looking forward to the next two seasons, but Bernie had other plans.

2

Rookie

There really wasn't any reason for Bernie to stay in school, either academically or athletically. Through a combination of college-credit courses that he had taken while he was still in high school, a heavy college course load, and credits from summer school, Bernie would be able to graduate in July, after only three years at Miami.

Athletically he had already proven himself to be the best quarterback in the college ranks. There were no obstacles and nothing left to prove. "I felt like I had reached a certain level there. I felt I wasn't progressing at the rate I could be." If he wanted to accelerate his development as a quarterback, there was only one place to do it—the NFL.

After Bernie made his announcement, a lot of teams tried to get in a position to obtain his draft rights. There were some NFL talent scouts, though, who doubted his abilities.

Mike Hickey of the Jets was the most vocal doubter. "I question whether Kosar is as good as some people make him out to be. Exactly how mobile is he? Exactly how strong is his arm? How good are his mechanics?"

Everyone is entitled to his opinion, and Hickey wasn't the only doubter; but it is instructive to remember that Hickey is the man who bypassed Dan Marino in the 1983 draft in favor of Ken O'Brien.

Gil Brandt, the vice president of the Dallas Cowboys, had a different assessment of Bernie's abilities. "He gets the ball to the right man at the right time. Joe Montana doesn't have a particularly strong arm, and he's done some pretty good things. What we do is put too much emphasis on height, too much on speed, and we forget the guys who get the job done."

George Young, the general manager of the Giants, has a very simple approach for rating quarterbacks. "You can learn what you need to know about a quarterback by watching him in a two-minute drill. The great ones know how to throw all the necessary passes. They retain their composure. They lead and others follow.

"No doubt about it," Young said for emphasis. "The kid has shown he can do it."

Bernie's status as a three-year graduate allowed him to enter a special supplemental draft. The Cleveland Browns traded four draft picks, including two number ones, to the Buffalo Bills for the right to make Bernie the number one pick in the supplemental draft. Ernie Accorsi, the man who directs the Browns' football operations, in explaining why he was willing to give up so much to sign Bernie, spoke about his resemblance to ex-Colt Hall-of-Famer John Unitas. "It's that personality of relentless defiance. They will not accept defeat."

The hometown boy was coming home. When Bernie signed his contract, he smiled and said, "This is what I've always wanted."

Even before Bernie arrived in training camp, he was being hailed as a hero by the fans and the news media. Reporters kept trying to get Bernie to open up, but he is a very private person and doesn't enjoy the public spotlight. When pressed to answer questions, Bernie gives the impression that he'd rather be visiting his dentist.

"People mean well. It's not that they bother me. It's that they want to talk about me and football, and those are two subjects that I find boring to talk about. And it doesn't get you anywhere as far as winning football games is concerned."

Bernie's rookie season was like a roller-coaster ride—lots of ups and downs and plenty of heart-pounding excitement. His first NFL start came in a preseason game against the Philadelphia Eagles, and it proved to be a rough introduction. He connected on only six of 22 attempts for 97 yards, threw an interception, and coughed up a fumble. Welcome to the NFL!

Bernie kept on practicing and didn't get discouraged. As he

said, "Each day you get better or worse. You never stay the same, and I have no intention of getting worse."

When the season began, though, veteran signal caller Gary Danielson was at the controls. Bernie had no argument. "Gary is definitely the best quarterback on the team right now. Progress hasn't been as fast as I wanted."

But in the second quarter of the fifth game Danielson, who had become Bernie's best friend on the team, went down with a shoulder injury.

The fans in Cleveland Stadium cheered as Bernie ran onto the field. He ducked in behind center to take his first NFL snap, called out the signals, and then—fumbled. "I never dreamed on my first play I'd leave the ball on the ground."

After that bobbling beginning, though, Bernie settled down and at one stretch completed seven in a row on his way to a nine-for-15 day. More importantly, he keyed a five-play, 53-yard fourth-quarter drive with passes to Brian Brennan (33 yards) and Ozzie Newsome (ten yards) that led the Browns to a 24–20 victory over the New England Patriots. The win gave the Browns a 3–2 record and first place in the AFC Central Division.

After the game Bernie happily clutched a ball and told reporters, "I clipped it at the end of the game. Dad gets it."

Bernie's first regular-season start came the following week against Houston. The blitzing Oilers swarmed all over Bernie and limited his passing to 44 yards in the first half. As Mike Babb put it, "Man, he took some *hits*." But Bernie and the Browns neutralized the blitz in the second half and put 21 points on the scoreboard, including Bernie's first NFL TD toss, a 68-yarder to wide receiver Clarence Weathers. "We had tried the play in the first half, but I cut the pass pattern," Weathers said. "Bernie came up to me on the sidelines afterwards and told me I could beat the guy long—he was right."

Bernie ran around slapping the hand of every Browns player in sight. "It's a lot of fun out there," he told reporters with a grin. But when asked about his performance, Bernie turned serious. "My performance was acceptable. The main thing is we won."

Bernie's dad was a bit more excited. "Bernie was awesome. He took a lot of pops, but he's tough—like his mother. He always finds a way to get the job done."

The Browns had trouble with their offense in their next game, against the L.A. Raiders, and trailed 14–7 at halftime. Late in the game, though, Bernie drilled a seven-yard TD pass to running back Kevin Mack to give Cleveland a 20–13 lead.

But the Raiders rallied, and with only 29 seconds left in the game, tight end Todd Christensen pulled in a scoring pass to steal the game away. The roller coaster had taken a sudden, unexpected dip, and Bernie had tasted his first NFL loss.

Washington came to Cleveland to give Bernie his next test. He threw an interception on their first possession, and the fans began to boo. He botched a handoff on the second series, and the boos grew louder. On the third series Bernie threw another interception, and the fans were getting hoarse as Washington led 14–0. When the second half began, Bernie was on the bench; he had flunked this test. Coach Marty Schottenheimer decided to rely on Danielson. Bernie was upset at being yanked. "I wanted to stay in there. I was pretty disappointed."

The Browns traveled to Three Rivers Stadium, where they lost for the sixteenth consecutive time. Bernie was back as the starting QB, and he hit on eight straight passes and 13 of 19, but they gained only 96 yards and no TD's. The Browns also lost their poise when they let the hooting of the Steeler fans disrupt their signal calling. Five consecutive times Bernie had to back away from the center when a wave of booing washed down on the field, and the team became rattled.

Cleveland's next game was against Cincinnati, and the folks in Riverfront Stadium were ready. Thousands of miniature megaphones stenciled with the words "Bernie Blaster" were handed out as the crowd tried to taunt Bernie by reminding him of the incident in Pittsburgh.

Bernie claimed that the blasters didn't bother him, but he was upset with his second-half passing, which totaled two for nine with two interceptions. "I'm not happy with performances like that," he said after the 27–10 loss.

Bernie was reminded that rookie quarterbacks were expected to have rough times. "What other people do or do not expect doesn't enter into it. I expect a lot from my abilities. I expect a lot from myself."

Just when it seemed like the Browns might not win again, they beat Buffalo 17–7 to improve their record to 5–6. The game didn't produce any plays for the highlights tape, but Bernie did manage a fourth-quarter TD toss that gave the Browns some breathing room.

The Bengals came to town the following week, and Coach Schottenheimer elected to start Danielson despite his sore shoulder. Gary's shoulder was so sore that he was only able to throw one pass in the second half, but the pass broke the game open and provided Cleveland with an important victory.

After the game Bengals' Coach Sam Wyche was asked about the difference between the two quarterbacks. "I don't want to knock Kosar, but Danielson's experience was important on that big touchdown. He knew that he was going to get hit, but he threw the ball perfectly."

As one of Bernie's teammates observed, "You can't replace experience with anything."

Bernie started the next game, against the Giants, but he was ineffective (six of 16 for only 86 yards). Danielson came on in relief again and led the Browns to an exciting 35–33 come-from-behind victory by directing two scoring drives in the final twelve minutes.

Bernie was happy for his friend but disappointed about not being allowed to finish the game. Danielson downplayed the situation. "I just go game to game. Bernie's the future, the franchise."

Schottenheimer said that he had put Gary in for his experience. "Gary's smart. He's a winner, and we needed to win that game."

After a loss to the Seahawks the Browns needed a win over the Oilers to stay in contention for the division title. Bernie responded with his best performance of the season and led the Browns to a 28–21 victory. Bernie played error-free football, throwing for three TD's and running for a fourth.

Ozzie Newsome, who caught his 500th career pass during the game (only the fourteen player in NFL history to reach that milestone), was beaming about Bernie's performance. "Bernie will just get better and better. Anytime an athlete has hard times, he needs a confidence builder. This game could do it for Bernie. He has never let any team down that he has been on."

Reporters didn't ask Bernie about the three TD passes or the fact that he hadn't thrown an interception in his last 112 attempts. They didn't even ask if he had felt pressure playing in a game that Cleveland had to win. Everyone was more interested in talking about the two-yard bootleg he had run in for the TD.

"We usually run the backs up the middle in that situation," Bernie explained, "so it was a good deviation. It should have been easier to run it in," he smiled, "but with my blazing speed, I made it real close.

"I expect performances like today. I really enjoy getting up for these important games. We have a lot of rookies on this team, but now we're getting experience."

But the enjoyment only lasted until the following week, when the Browns traveled to New Jersey and experienced a clobbering by the Jets, 37–10.

Mark Gastineau, Joe Klecko, and friends unleashed a devastating pass rush that sacked Bernie twice and caused him to cough up two fumbles. The Jets also picked off a pass, breaking Bernie's streak at 134 consecutive attempts without an interception.

Despite their dispirited play, the Browns—with an 8–8 record —did manage to back into the divisional title. They became the first NFL team to make the play-offs without a winning record.

Bernie, however, wasn't concerned with Cleveland's record or the fact that they would be facing Dan Marino and the Dolphins in his first play-off game. "I'm looking forward to going back to Miami. This type of opportunity is what I want," he said firmly.

Bernie celebrated his return to the Orange Bowl, the scene of his greatest triumphs, by leading the Browns on an opening-quarter, ten-play, 82-yard drive, which he capped with a 16-yard strike to Ozzie Newsome.

Two long touchdown runs by Earnest Byner and a stingy defense increased Cleveland's lead to 21–3 in the third quarter. But Marino rallied Miami, and they closed the gap to 21–17 with two quick touchdowns. With time running out, Cleveland had a third down and two at the Miami 48. If they made the first down, they might be able to run out the clock, but Curtis Dickey was dropped for a six-yard loss. The Dolphins, given an opportunity, took control and punched across the score that gave them a 24–21 victory.

The Browns had thrown only 19 passes, most of them short routes, while they rushed 37 times. Bernie was upset. He had gotten the opportunity to play the game, but he didn't get the chance to run the offense at full throttle. "We need to improve our passing philosophy. It's not at a professional level. We need to loosen up and take it to them. But," he reminded the reporters, "we're young; we'll be back."

The roller coaster had come to a stop. It had been a bumpy ride.

3

Almost There

Bernie came to training camp in 1986 filled with optimism about the upcoming season. The dramatic play-off loss to Miami had hurt. "We were up eighteen points, and you should never lose a game if you have that significant a lead," observed Bernie. But Bernie wasn't going to let it stifle him. "A lot of people look at the Dolphin game as an end, but I think it's a beginning. We're growing."

Bernie was also pleased that the Browns had hired Lindy Infante as their offensive coordinator. He was the offensive innovator who had helped the Bengals develop a high-powered passing attack, one that had been strong enough to lead the Bengals into Super Bowl XVI.

A lot of people questioned whether Bernie had enough experience to lead the Browns to the next level. Gary Danielson didn't have any doubts. "He has an overall feel for things on the field. He knows when to look away from his primary receiver; he can feel a blitz coming and feel when it's only being faked. He plays football like Isaiah Thomas plays basketball. He knows where everyone is."

The schedule maker provided an opening-day test for Bernie and the Browns—the Super Bowl champion Bears in Chicago. The Monsters of the Midway steamrolled to three early touchdowns, including a 58-yard interception return by linebacker Wilbur Marshall. Down by 21–7 in the first quarter, the Browns could have crumbled right then; but they didn't.

Bernie led them on a 72-yard scoring drive in the second quarter and then added another score on the opening series of the second half. After Chicago had stretched the lead to 34–24, Bernie cranked it up again and hit Brian Brennan with a 15-yard score to shrink the gap to 34–31 with just under six minutes left in the game.

Chicago wound up winning the game 41–31, but it was clear that Cleveland and its young quarterback had taken a large step toward joining the ranks of the NFL elite. Bears Coach Mike Ditka was impressed with Bernie. "He's darn good." And Richard Dent, Chicago's great pass rusher, added, "We thought he couldn't scramble, but he scrambled. He got the ball away."

When asked about the fierce blitz of the Bears, Bernie just shrugged. "You can't worry about the rush coming in. But you do develop a sense of where it's coming from." You also develop a sense of how to get some help. As offensive tackle Rickey Bolden put it, "He's matured so much since last year. He really kept his composure. When their rush kept forcing him to throw too soon, he told us, 'Hey, I have to have time back there.' He sounded like a veteran."

Coach Schottenheimer was still bothered by the inconsistency of his young quarterback. "But," he noted, "Bernie doesn't let the mistakes bother him. There is a mental toughness about him. That's going to be a big factor in his development. That's why he'll be an outstanding quarterback."

And how did Bernie react to compiling career-best statistics for passes attempted (40), completed (23), and yardage (283), as well as a scrapbookful of praise? "We lost the game. A lot of people were pleased by the effort, but not the players. Our goal is to win, and we didn't play well enough to win."

Bernie pulled out the next game when he hit Reggie Langhorne with a 55-yard scoring pass with 2:10 left to give the Browns a 13–9 victory over the Oilers. Then after a loss to the Bengals they strung together three consecutive victories, including their first win ever at Three Rivers Stadium.

After the streak was interrupted by a disappointing loss to the lowly Packers, the Browns ran off three straight again. They began the streak with an exciting come-from-behind victory over the

Vikings and continued it with an easy victory over the Colts in which Bernie threw three TD passes to three different receivers, including a 72-yarder to Ray Fontenot.

The long passing game had begun developing. The offense had been opened up and no longer relied solely on the run and short-passing game. Bernie was happy, and the Browns were winning.

The third game in the streak was a Monday nighter against the Dolphins on national TV, their first meeting since the play-off game. The coaches took the wraps off the passing game and turned Bernie loose. He responded with 32 completions in 50 attempts for 401 yards, all career highs, and Cleveland clobbered Miami 26–16. The coaches had finally unhitched the thoroughbred from the cart and let him run.

Bernie praised his linemen for the job they had done in keeping him safe from the big nasties on the other team. "The line was the main factor," he said with typical modesty. "When they give you that kind of security in the pocket, it makes life a lot easier."

Bernie wasn't bothered about becoming the first man in NFL history to throw for 400 yards without tossing a TD. "We needed this game to stay in first place. That's the main thing. A quarterback gets his personal satisfaction from winning."

The winning streak, however, came to a halt against the rowdy Raiders. Bernie went from being showered with praise to soaking his bruises as the Raiders sacked him six times and beat the Browns 27–17. Raider coach Tom Flores had seen what Bernie had done to Miami the previous week and turned his rush loose. "He just picked them apart. We knew we couldn't give him a lot of time. We just went after him."

The following week produced one of the most exciting games of the season as the Browns pulled out a 37–31 overtime victory over the Steelers. Bernie had another sensational day as he went 28 for 46 for 414 yards and two TD's. The game winner was a 36-yard TD toss to wide receiver Brian Brennan. "When we came up to the line of scrimmage, Bernie saw that they were in a blitz and he gave me a fist, which means I go long. Bernie put it right on the money. All I had to do was catch it.''

Bernie explained that when the defense blitzes, it forces the offense to react quickly or suffer a sack, but it also makes the defense vulnerable because they've weakened their pass coverage. ''You have to have a good sense of timing, and you have to be able to get rid of the ball quickly. All eleven guys have to be on the same page—the pass protection, the receivers making the necessary adjustments on the pass routes, and the quarterback getting rid of the ball.''

Coach Chuck Noll, who had coached Terry Bradshaw and led the Steelers to four Super Bowls, was impressed. ''He has a remarkable ability to look one way and quickly throw in another direction. He's come a long way. He's the kind of player who can carry a team.''

The offense went from high gear to neutral in their next two games, but they managed to win both, 13–10 at home against Houston in overtime and 21–14 in Buffalo on a cold and windy day as Bernie and the Bills' Jim Kelly faced each other for the first time since their days at the University of Miami. The windy weather had been a factor in both games. ''You need to be patient if there's a bad throw or a dropped pass,'' explained a quickly maturing Bernie Kosar. ''You need so much concentration. Nothing out there was easy.''

The Browns came out blasting against the Bengals in the next game, as they looked to wrap up their second-straight AFC Central Division title. Bernie began by hitting Reggie Langhorne with a 66-yard strike that set up a short TD burst by Kevin Mack on the first series. Bernie rang up another score when he tossed a 47-yarder to Webster Slaughter, and the Browns went on to smash the Bengals 34–3. Afterward Bernie explained why the Browns had played with such intensity. ''They had humiliated us on national TV earlier this year. We wanted this game.''

Cleveland closed out the regular season with a 47–17 blowout of the San Diego Chargers as Bernie completed 21 of 28 while throwing for 258 yards and two TD's in three quarters of playing time.

Bernie had taken great strides as a quarterback and team leader. He had improved his statistics dramatically, but most importantly he had led the Browns to the best record in the AFC, 12–4, and the most wins in the history of the franchise.

The play-offs, though, started a new season, and the regular-season stats and victories didn't count. In the play-offs everyone starts even, and every game is sudden death.

The game between the Browns and the Jets seemed to be a mismatch, a contest between teams headed in opposite directions. Cleveland had finished with the best record in the AFC and a five-game winning streak, while the Jets just barely made the play-offs as a wild-card team after *losing* their last five games. What it turned out to be, however, was one of the most exciting play-off games ever and the third-longest game in NFL history.

The Jets opened the scoring with a flea flicker, but the Browns bounced back when Bernie connected with Fontenot on a 37-yard TD. Then the scoring slackened off as the offenses stumbled and the defenses asserted themselves. The Jets nursed a 13–10 lead into the fourth quarter and, after intercepting a pass, stretched their lead to 20–10 with only 4:14 left in the game.

At that point, according to Brian Brennan, ''Bernie took us aside and said, 'We can win this game. Don't give up.''' Then Bernie cranked up his right arm and connected on five consecutive passes to position Kevin Mack's one-yard TD burst. But Cleveland still trailed 20–17, and there was only a minute and 57 seconds left in their season.

The Cleveland defense did its job and forced the Jets to punt, and the Browns now had one last opportunity and just over one minute left to prolong their season. In two quick plays—a penalty against the Jets and a 37-yard strike to Webster Slaughter—the Browns moved the ball to the Jets' 15-yard line. With only seven seconds left, Mark Moseley came into the game and kicked a 22-yard field goal to send the game into overtime.

In the sudden-death period Bernie led the Browns on a drive to the Jets' five-yard line. On first down Schottenheimer sent Moseley in to win the game, but as the Browns' fans moaned, he missed the 23-yard attempt.

The game wore on and the players wore down, and the Browns began another drive on their 31-yard line. The Jets, trying to protect against Bernie's passes—he had already equaled the play-off record with 33 pass completions and established new records for attempts (64) and yardage (489)—replaced some of their linebackers with smaller, lighter defensive backs. But the Browns realized what the strategy of the Jets was, and completely crossed them up. Seven straight times they ran the ball against the Jets' defense that was designed to deal with the threat of Bernie's passing. With Kevin Mack piling up most of the yardage, Cleveland moved relentlessly down the field to the Jets' nine-yard line. Once again Schottenheimer sent Moseley in to kick, and this time his kick sailed through the uprights and lifted Cleveland to a heart-pounding 23–20 win.

"I've never experienced or seen a comeback like that," said a happy and relieved Schottenheimer. "Bernie Kosar is a championship player."

Reporters wanted to know if Bernie had been shaken up by the two fourth-quarter interceptions that he had thrown. "I didn't lose my confidence. I didn't want to leave the field being remembered for the interceptions. And four minutes seemed like enough time."

Moseley, the old veteran, pointed to Bernie and said, "After two interceptions a lot of quarterbacks would have started talking to themselves." Ozzie Newsome summed it up best, though, when he said, "The Jets were much tougher than we expected. But Bernie took us down. He got that look in his eye, and we all knew that he could do it."

There really wasn't any time to sit and savor their victory, though, because they had to try to do it all over again the following week against John Elway and the Denver Broncos.

The Browns played a ragtag game against the Broncos. They turned the ball over three times in the first half—two interceptions and a fumble—and squandered numerous opportunities. But the Broncos hadn't capitalized on all of their chances, either, so when Bernie hit on his second TD pass, a 48-yarder to Brian Brennan, Cleveland had the lead 20–13 with only 5:43 left. It seemed that the Browns, despite their sloppy play, would squeeze out a victory.

But John Elway engineered one of the greatest drives in the history of postseason play as he led his team 98 yards to tie the score with only 37 ticks left on the clock.

Cleveland won the toss and had the first chance to score in the sudden-death overtime. But they came up short when they tried a run on a third down and two. Eyebrows were raised by Schottenheimer's decision to try the run instead of letting Bernie pass for the first down.

After the punt Elway once again led the Broncos into scoring position, and Rich Karlis kicked the field goal that brought Cleveland's dream season to a nightmarish end.

4

Instant Replay

If Bernie's first season was like a roller-coaster ride, his second season was like tumbling off a mountain one step from the top. Bernie was bothered by the loss, but he didn't let it weigh him down. "I went over that game a lot in the off-season. I think we'll learn from it. We had a very young team, and I think the experience of that type of pressure was good for us. I know that I enjoy that atmosphere."

It was that attitude and the added experience that had a lot of people talking Super Bowl for the Browns during the 1987 preseason. Bernie, though, ever practical, knew that first there was a schedule of games to play and a possible players' strike. "I don't want to think about a game that won't be played until the end of January. I don't think that any of us should. First we have to beat the Saints; they're real aggressive and won't beat themselves."

Bernie proved to be a prophet as New Orleans handed Cleveland its fifth-straight season-opening loss. Bernie showed that he was ready, though, by connecting on 28 passes good for 314 yards and two TD's, and even scored one himself. The Browns bounced back to beat the Steelers, but before their next game, a date with Denver, the NFL players' strike interrupted the season. The Denver game was canceled, and the next three games were played mostly with replacement players. Some teams, like Washington, stuck together, and none of their regulars played during the strike. But on other teams, like the Browns, some regulars did join the replacement players, and that caused bad feelings among team-mates. When the strike ended, Bernie demonstrated his leadership by trying to heal the wounds. He quickly shook hands with each of the players who had crossed the picket line and announced, "We have to put this behind us. We have to get ready for the rest of the season. If you worry about what happened, all it can do is hurt you in the long run.''

In the long run Bernie led the Browns to seven victories in their final ten games, including the last three, as they earned their third consecutive AFC Central Division title. Bernie had matured, both as a quarterback and as a team leader. Ozzie Newsome spoke about Bernie's quiet leadership. "He never changes. He's the same whether he's having a tough day or a great day. His stability rubs off on the rest of us.'' Wide receiver Reggie Langhorne summed up the feelings of the entire team when he said, ''He takes complete charge. Bottom line is, we believe in him.''

Todd Christensen, the Raiders' all-pro tight end, also noticed the big change in Bernie. "Last year when we blitzed, we confused him, knocked him down, and won easily. This year when we blitzed, he read them and made some big plays. There's a big difference. Kosar is as important to Cleveland as Elway is to Denver.''

Bernie's growth as a quarterback could also be seen in his statistics. He threw for at least one touchdown in every game, and he threw for more than 200 yards in all but two games. He led the AFC with a 95.4 quarterback rating and a 62.0 completion percentage, and his interception rate (2.3) was the second-best in the NFL.

More importantly, Bernie led a balanced Browns attack (482 rushing plays; 474 passing plays) that kept defenses guessing and produced an AFC-leading 390 points. Schottenheimer put it in perspective when he said, "His style will always be 'team first.' Some quarterbacks don't understand how important that is until late in their careers; some never do. We got a special one with Bernie.''

Cleveland's first opponent in the play-offs was Indianapolis, which had already beaten the Browns during the regular season.

Bernie got the Browns off the blocks quickly as he led them on a game-opening, 15-play, 86-yard drive that he finished off with a ten-yard TD toss to Earnest Byner. Eric Dickerson scored just before halftime to knot the score at 14–14, but the Browns put the game on ice with a 24-point second half. Bernie finished the game with 229 yards passing and three TD tosses while going 20 for 31. He had led the Browns up the mountain again; the next step was Denver, the mile-high city.

The thin Denver air crackled with electricity as the teams took the field for their AFC championship rematch. The expectations of a tight, tense duel seemed to evaporate early, though, as Denver, helped by two Cleveland miscues, took a 21–3 lead into the locker room.

But the contest was far from over. "We knew we didn't get this far by quitting," said Bernie, "and we didn't plan on selling out in the second half." The Browns didn't quit; they battled back behind two third-quarter TD tosses by Bernie that narrowed the gap to 31–24. Early in the fourth quarter, as Denver fans sat glumly in the stands at Mile High Stadium, Bernie directed another long drive. In nine plays he took the Browns 86 yards, including a 53-yard strike to Byner, and finished off with a five-yard TD toss to Webster Slaughter that tied the score at 31–31.

As Nick Buoniconti, the former all-pro middle linebacker, put it, "Kosar was completing passes like there was no defense on the field."

The top of the mountain was within reach.

John Elway knocked them down, though, as he rallied the Broncos with a TD pass to Sammy Winder to give them the lead again at 38–31 with only 4:01 left to play.

The stadium hummed with excitement as the Browns took over on their 35-yard line with just 3:53 left in the game. Everyone's thoughts flashed back to last year and The Drive. "I was figuring on overtime," confessed Elway. "Bernie was putting 'em up there faster than we could even count them."

Playing with great confidence, Bernie led the Browns down to the Denver eight-yard line. Then he handed the ball off to Byner, Cleveland's leading rusher and receiver during the game. Byner started up the middle, cut to the outside, and headed for the end zone. But Jeremiah Castille, a Denver defensive back, stripped the ball out of Byner's grasp at the two and pounced on the fumble that brought Cleveland's season to a sudden and agonizing conclusion.

Even in defeat Bernie still commanded admiration. Jim Ryan, Denver's leading tackler, spoke with open admiration, "Bernie Kosar is a phenomenal quarterback. I respected him before the game, but now I have an even deeper respect for him."

Ricky Hunley, another Denver linebacker, explained how difficult it had been to play against Bernie in the second half. "It was frustrating, very frustrating. He was hot. They were hitting on all cylinders. Every time we used a different defense, he had a different answer."

And Karl Mecklenberg, the Broncos' all-pro defenseman who has been John Elway's teammate for five years, added, "The way Kosar played in the second half was as good as any two quarters I've ever seen any quarterback play in my career."

Bernie, though, wasn't consoled either by the praise or the fact that he had completed an AFC title-game-record 26 passes good for 356 yards and three touchdowns; or that Cleveland's 31 points were the most ever scored in a championship game by a losing team. "It's no fun losing this game once," Bernie said, "much less two years in a row. We really believe we should have won."

But Bernie will bounce back. He has helped lead the Browns to the brink for two consecutive seasons, and there's no doubt that he is determined to take that final step to the Super Bowl. With his self-confidence, self-discipline, and willingness to work hard he's a good bet to get his wish. As Howard Schnellenberger, his former coach at Miami, observed, "I've worked with a lot of great quarterbacks with a lot of mental toughness, but I think that Bernie has it better than any of them. He's the kind of kid who has always achieved what he set out to achieve."

John Elway

COLLEGE STATISTICS

				Passing					Rushing		
	G	ATT	COMP	PCT	YDS	TD	INT	ATT	YDS	AVG	TD
1979	9	96	50	.521	544	6	3	26	51	1.9	0
1980	11	379	248	.654	2889	27	11	100	400	4.0	4
1981	11	366	214	.584	2674	20	13	74	201	2.7	1
1982	11	405	262	.647	3242	24	12	59	167	2.8	0
Totals	42	1246	774	.621	9349	77	39	259	819	3.2	5

NFL REGULAR SEASON

				Passing				QB		Rushing		
	G	ATT	COMP	PCT	YDS	TD	INT	RATG	ATT	YDS	AVG	TD
1983	11	259	123	47.5	1663	7	14	54.9	28	146	5.2	1
1984	15	380	214	56.3	2598	18	15	76.8	56	237	4.2	1
1985	16	605	327	54.0	3891	22	23	70.2	51	253	5.0	0
1986	16	504	280	55.6	3485	19	13	79.0	52	257	4.9	1
1987	12	410	224	54.6	3198	19	12	83.4	66	304	4.6	4
Totals	70	2158	1168	54.1	14835	85	77	74.1	253	1197	4.7	7

NFL POSTSEASON

				Passing				QB		Rushing		
	G	ATT	COMP	PCT	YDS	TD	INT	RATG	ATT	YDS	AVG	TD
1983	1	15	10	66.7	123	0	1	N/A	3	16	5.3	0
1984	1	37	19	51.3	184	2	2	N/A	4	16	4.0	0
1986	3	107	57	53.2	805	3	4	N/A	15	101	6.7	2
1987	3	89	42	47.1	797	6	5	N/A	18	76	4.2	0
Totals	8	248	128	51.6	1909	11	12	71.8	40	209	5.2	2

Bernie Kosar

*COLLEGE STATISTICS

			Passing					Rushing			
	G	ATT	COMP	PCT	YDS	TD	INT	ATT	YDS	AVG	TD
1983	11	327	201	61.4	2329	15	13	52	−156	−3.0	4
1984	12	416	262	63	3642	25	16	52	−230	−4.4	4
Totals	23	743	463	62.3	5971	40	29	104	−386	−3.71	8
Orange Bowl 1983		35	19	54.2	300	2	1	2	−7	−3.5	0
Fiesta Bowl 1984		44	31	70.4	294	2	1	8	−24	−3.0	0

NFL REGULAR SEASON

			Passing						Rushing			
	G	ATT	COMP	PCT	YDS	TD	INT	QB RATG	ATT	YDS	AVG	TD
1985	12	248	124	50.0	1578	8	7	69.3	26	−12	−0.5	1
1986	16	531	310	58.4	3854	17	10	83.8	24	19	0.8	0
1987	12	389	241	62.0	3033	22	9	95.4	15	22	1.5	1
Totals	40	1168	675	57.8	8465	47	26	84.6	65	39	0.6	2

NFL POSTSEASON

			Passing						Rushing			
	G	ATT	COMP	PCT	YDS	TD	INT	QB RATG	ATT	YDS	AVG	TD
1985	1	19	10	52.6	166	1	1	N/A	2	6	3.0	0
1986	2	96	51	53.1	748	3	4	N/A	5	3	0.6	0
1987	2	72	46	63.8	685	6	2	N/A	1	5	5.0	0
Totals	5	187	107	57.2	1499	10	7	83.2	8	14	1.8	0

*The college rushing statistics include plays on which Bernie was sacked. That explains the negative yardage figures.

JOHN ELWAY—1988 RECORD SHEET

GAME	OPPONENT	SCORE	WIN OR LOSE	Passing								Rushing			
				COMP	ATT	PCT	YDS	INT	TD	ATT	YDS	AVG	TD
1													
2													
3													
4													
5													
6													
7													
8													
9													
10													
11													
12													
13													
14													
15													
16													
TOTALS													
PLAY-OFF GAME													
PLAY-OFF GAME													
PLAY-OFF GAME													
SUPER BOWL													
TOTALS													

BERNIE KOSAR—1988 RECORD SHEET

GAME	OPPONENT	SCORE	WIN OR LOSE	Passing						Rushing			
				COMP	ATT	PCT	YDS	INT	TD	ATT	YDS	AVG	TD
1													
2													
3													
4													
5													
6													
7													
8													
9													
10													
11													
12													
13													
14													
15													
16													
TOTALS													
PLAY-OFF GAME													
PLAY-OFF GAME													
PLAY-OFF GAME													
SUPER BOWL													
TOTALS													